W9-DJL-118

understanding your

cat

understanding your

cat

An illustrated guide to understanding your cat

Don Harper

This is a Parragon Publishing book
This edition published in 2005

Parragon Publishing
Queen Street House
4 Queen Street
Bath BA1 1HE, UK

Copyright © Parragon 2001

All rights reserved. No part of this publication may be reproduced, stored in a retrieval system, or transmitted in any form or by any means, electronic, mechanical, photocopying, recording, or otherwise, without the prior permission of the copyright holder.

Created and produced by The Bridgewater Book Company Ltd.

Cover by Talking Design

Artists John Woodcock, Patricia Clements, Alan Male

ISBN 1-40545-809-7

Printed in China

contents

introducing **cats**

From the magnificent tiger to the humble pet cat, few creatures in the animal world are more recognizable than cats. Cats have been closely associated with people for several thousand years, and yet the cats we keep today as pets have never sacrificed their independent natures as a result of being domesticated.

As wild predators, cats have evolved ways of hunting and surviving. These same characteristics can be seen in our own domestic cats. From time to time, most of us will see how our own cat's behavior mirrors that of its wild relatives. Even today, the independent nature of cats means that they are quite capable of reverting back to a wild existence within a generation or so. We only have to look at feral cats to realize how this can be the case.

We have domesticated cats for a variety of reasons. The traditional role of the cat in our society was to control pests, although few will be expected to do this today. Some purebred cats are kept for breeding and showing. But most of our cats are kept as pets, for pleasure and companionship. Having a pet—such as a cat, or a dog—has been shown to have well-known advantages to humans in terms of reducing stress, and living longer and healthier lives.

All colors of domestic cat are descended from the tabby markings of their ancestors.

The tiger (Panthera tigris) is the only striped wild cat species. In many ways it shares behavioral characteristics with our own domestic cats. It is a solitary hunter, who roams a territory for food, and spends much of the day asleep.

Of course taking on a pet is a major decision. Your cat is likely to remain with you for up to 15 years, or longer. By the end of that time, young children may have grown up, or your circumstances may have changed considerably. This means you have to make some serious decisions about what sort of cat you buy and if you can provide a long-term home for it. In return, you will have a pet that is independent, elegant, clean, and affectionate, and with whom many owners feel privileged to share a living space.

The mystery of cats

One of the things that has always intrigued people about cats is their mystery. Even after centuries of domestication, a cat can still remain aloof and somewhat secretive. Although your cat seems to need you, you may feel that you never really get to know your cat in the same way as you get to know your dog. You will never be able to train your cat to bring your paper to you in the morning, or your slippers to you late at night, as your dog may do. There are times that you may feel you do not understand your cat very well, and indeed, many people frequently misinterpret their cat's behavior. It may be hard to understand why a cat sprays in the home, for instance, unless you realize how important scent-marking is in its territory.

Understanding the cat

Cats are less openly expressive than dogs; they are quieter and appear to be less demanding of us. To help us understand cats as pets we have to be more aware of a cat's body language—the ears and tail are both expressive parts of a cat's body. The eyes and whiskers too tell us about a cat's feelings and its state of mind. Purring, chirruping, and meowing are all sounds a cat makes that we can begin to understand if we watch and listen carefully. A cat's scent, sounds, and body language are the most important means of communication with us and with each other.

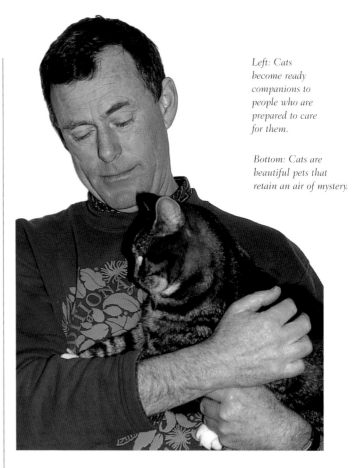

Left: Cats become ready companions to people who are prepared to care for them.

Bottom: Cats are beautiful pets that retain an air of mystery.

Some cats are very vocal, and owners soon learn to understand what their cats are trying to tell them.

We treat our cats as members of the family our cats have a name, a home, food, a bed, and we care about their happiness and well-being. Understanding a cat's behavior—be it a kitten or a cat who has shared your home for many years—is rewarding because it enriches your relationship with your pet and provides greater enjoyment for both.

So what do you do if you want to own a cat? If you are thinking of getting a cat, but have not yet started to look you will find that the ease of finding the cat of your choice depends partly on what you are looking for. If you are determined to locate a particular breed and variety of purebred cat, reading advertisements in cat magazines, searching the Internet, visiting shows, and contacting the national cat registration bodies are all ways in which it is possible to locate breeders. Pedigree kittens are usually ready to go to new homes when they are 12 weeks old. Kittens who are not purebred may be found through friends or other reliable sources, and can usually be transferred to new surroundings at a slightly younger age than purebred cats, but never sooner than eight weeks.

When looking at a litter of kittens, it is difficult to determine their temperaments. At the time of your visit, one kitten may appear to be more lively than another, having just woken up for example, but it is better to be guided more by the advice of the breeder. Even so, there is usually little to choose between kittens in a litter at this stage, because they have all had a similar background. What is most important is to select a healthy kitten at the outset. Beware of any litters where kittens have runny eyes or noses, or display staining under the tail, which may indicate diarrhea. The kittens should not look thin, especially when this is combined with a potbellied appearance, which can indicate that the kittens have a problem with worms. It is definitely not a good idea to obtain the weakest member of a litter because this could turn out to be a sickly individual, who would then be likely to need on-going veterinary care.

Temperament

There are general differences between the various breeds of cats in terms of personality, but overall, much of a cat's temperament will be shaped by its exposure to people, especially in the first few weeks of its life when socialization takes place. It is also important to start out with a new

Silver tabby kittens. Be guided by what the breeder says about the temperaments of individual kittens in the litter.

kitten at a time when you are likely to be at home during the day, or certainly at a stage when you will be able to give your new pet plenty of attention.

Left: Bonds can form between dogs and cats as well as between cats and people.

Any other members of the household should also take a role in caring for the young cat, to prevent it developing into a one-person cat, attached only to you.

Cats can form very strong bonds with those in their immediate circle, despite the fact that in the wild they normally live solitary lifestyles. Sometimes, this bond can be formed with a puppy as much as a person, particularly if the kitten arrives at the same time as the young dog. But it is not a good idea to leave a kitten on its own unsupervised with a dog at first. Even if it does not cause any direct physical harm, the dog may well scare the cat and this might cause long-term problems.

Giving a cat a good home

If you are taking on an older cat, it is helpful to know something about its background in order to make the right choice of cat to suit your circumstances. Also, it may not be as easy to insure a cat of an unknown age and background, compared with a young kitten. However, there are many older cats that are in need of good homes and it makes sense to look at the different options available. If you already own another cat, the new cat needs to be introduced carefully. When you bring a new kitten home, it should have been wormed, inoculated, and have had a general health checkup. Looked after with care and an understanding of a cat's needs, this should be the start of a rewarding relationship and a great deal of fun.

Everyone in a family can have a role in giving a cat time and attention.

Cats often have both the stability of a home and the freedom to roam in a territory.

A cat's basic nature

1

When you look at your cat, what do you see—a domesticated pet—a well-loved member of the family? But can you also see the ways in which your cat has quite similar behavior to its wild relatives? When a cat pounces, it readily shows that it is a predator. When it leaps from a wall or climbs a tree, it shows it has natural agility. When it plays, jumps, or climbs up a frame, it shows off its natural reflexes. When it marks trees with its claws and its scent, it shows it is territorial. All these characteristics are like those of its ancestors and other wild predators. Maybe your cat is solitary, affectionate toward the people it knows, but wary of strangers? This is a bit like the bonds between wildcats. Your cat may be tame, but wherever there are domestic cats, there may well be groups of feral cats living together who have reverted to a wild state, even in city areas. So how domesticated are our cats—and can we discover their true nature?

evolution
of wildcats

To trace the evolution of the cat, we have to go back about 65 million years ago to the time when the dinosaurs were dying out. The creodonts had evolved. They were predatory mammals whose name comes from the Greek words "kreas" meaning flesh and "odontos" meaning tooth. Some groups of creodonts were as large as bears of today, while other groups (such as *Hyaenodon*) were small and athletic, with long slender legs that enabled them to pursue prey. About 55 million years ago, at the beginning of the Eocene era, a group of successful predators called the miacids replaced the creodonts. Among the early miacids were the nimravids, who survived until 8 million years ago. They had long bodies and short legs and their canine teeth in their upper jaws made them one of the first of the "saber-toothed" cats.

Nimravus was one of the first of the "saber-toothed" cats. Although no one can be sure, it is quite possible that it had coat markings that are fairly similar to those of modern cats.

Nimravus itself grew to about 4ft. (1.2m) long and, like today's cats, had binocular vision to assist its hunting abilities. It could draw its sharp claws back into sheaths, like most wildcats today, and is believed to have hunted small prey such as birds by stalking them.

Smilodon

Saber-toothed tigers were among the most fearsome of the early cats, with their upper canines developed into enlarged saber-like daggers, which they used alongside their sharp claws to drag down and kill their prey. The remains of a number of different types of these cats have been discovered, of which the best known is Smilodon. It was about the size of a modern-day lion, with a powerful head, strong forelegs, and a short tail. It is likely that Smilodon lived and hunted in groups, like lions today.

Smilodon fed off great herds of grazing animals that roamed the continents. Its mouth was dominated by canine teeth which looked like tusks.

The distant ancestors of modern wildcats first appeared about 20 million years ago. Little is known about them, partly because they lived in forested areas, which do not leave us strong fossilized evidence. The fossils we have found of wildcats date from about 2 million years ago. The range of many wildcats of today is far smaller than in prehistoric times, when continents had not yet reached their current positions. This meant that cheetahs, for example, now confined to Africa, were once found in North America.

Below: The body shape of all wildcats is similar, as shown by this panther.

Miacids

Miacids were the ancestors of mammals such as
- the dog
- the bear
- the mongoose
- the raccoon.

Lions, too, ranged over a much wider area and, like cheetahs, crossed what is now the Bering Strait. During the last Ice Age (around 30,000 years ago) a land-bridge linked eastern Asia and western North America, allowing wildcats to move freely. As lions spread, so they diversified. The cave lion, which evolved in Europe, was the largest member of the cat family ever known, growing up to 11ft. 6in. (3.5m) in length. It survived until about 2,000 years ago, when its last stronghold was in the Balkan area of southeastern Europe.

Above: Once widely found in Europe, Africa, and southern Asia, the lion is now confined mainly to Africa and northwest India.

The cave lion, a larger version of today's lions, was probably the first wildcat to become extinct as a result of human persecution.

Rare cats

Today, other wildcats are now very rare. If they are not successfully conserved, many of today's larger surviving species, including the tiger and the Asian lion, now face a similar fate. These bigger wildcats need large habitats in which to roam, and unfortunately, with human settlement encroaching on their territories, there is less space for them to live. Also, although most wildcats are in theory protected, enforcing such legislation is difficult.

the cat family today

Today there are 37 surviving species of wildcats, living naturally on all the world's continents except Australia. The largest species is the tiger (*Panthera tigris*), the only wildcat with a striped coat pattern. The Siberian race is the heaviest, weighing up to 700lb. (320kg).

Habitats and camouflage

While most cats are solitary by nature, lions (*Panthera leo*) live in groups called prides. The size of the pride depends on how much food is available. Where prey is easily found and caught, the pride will be a larger group. Today, there are still a large number of lions found widely across Africa, but there are only about 250 lions left in Asia, where they are found only in the Gir Forest area of India.

Many cats live in such forested areas, where they can rely on forest cover to stalk their prey, and can also hide away from danger. Their attractive coat markings have a practical purpose, helping to camouflage the cat by breaking up the outline of its body. The black panther (*Panthera pardus*) is actually a leopard with a black coat—if you look closely, the cat's darker spotted patterning is visible.

The rare snow leopard inhabits parts of the Himalayas, where its pale-colored coat helps to camouflage its presence.

The tiger's range extends from areas of hot tropical forest in Thailand, north into parts of Siberia where snowfalls are common.

Today's Species

Cat groupings

The cat family can be grouped in different ways. Four distinctive groups can be identified as follows:

PANTHERA	**ACINONYX**
The jaguar, leopard, tiger, and lion.	The cheetah.
NEOFELIS	**FELIS**
The clouded leopard.	The lynx, puma, Pallas's cat, the wildcat, and the domestic cat.

Bobcats are native to North America and are so-called because of their short tails.

Black panthers tend to live in forested parts of the leopard's range. While many wildcats are found within the tropics, some are found in much more hostile places. The snow leopard (*Panthera uncia*) has a coat that is not only very thick, but is also very pale. This helps it blend in against the background of its native habitat, where there is snow lying on the ground for much of the year. As with many wildcats, very little is known about the lifestyle of the snow leopard because of its secretive nature. Some species of wildcat such as the Iriomote cat (*Felis iriomotensis*) were not discovered until very recently. This cat was found on Iriomote Island off the coast of Japan in the 1960s. It is very rare so there are probably fewer than one hundred of these cats in existence.

The black panther is a black-coated form of the leopard with a recessive black gene.

Wildcats have traditionally been split into big and small cats. This is based not so much on their size as on their vocalizations. Whereas large cats such as tigers and lions roar, only small cats purr. A lion's roar is the loudest sound made by any cat—registering at nearly 115 decibels in volume; it helps to keep members of the pride in touch with each other.

Wildcats compared

Although the body shape of wild cats is broadly similar, wildcats are not hard to recognize. Some have tufted ears, but tail length often varies. The bobcat (*Lynx rufus*) originates in North America and has the shortest tail of the cat family. Most cats are nocturnal, hunting from dusk onward, aided by their excellent nighttime vision. The cheetah (*Acinonyx jubatus*), has adapted to hunt by means of its speed. It is the fastest land mammal, capable of reaching speeds of up to 62mph. (100kph) in short bursts. Other wildcats can be equally athletic pumas (*Felis concolor*), for example, can leap distances of nearly 40ft. (12m) in a single bound.

wildcats
and hybrids

Since all wildcats share a common ancestor, it is not clear whether the cats that evolved on the continents of Europe and Africa are different forms of the same species, or if they should be regarded as completely separate species.

African and European cats

Wild cats occur over a huge area of Africa and Europe, and there are differences in their size and color throughout the range. Those living in arid areas have lighter, more sandy-colored coats than those living in forested areas. The coats of African wildcats are also shorter and sleeker than those of their European relatives, simply because the climate where they live is warmer. Their tails are usually longer, suggesting that they may climb more often (the tail is important to help the cat balance when it is jumping, climbing trees or clambering through branches).

Friend or foe?

African cats were found to be more friendly than the European cats. It may well have been for this reason that they were the first cats to be domesticated. Once domestic cats had been introduced to Europe and Asia, they soon started to crossbreed with the European wildcats.

Pallas's cat from Asia was thought to have contributed to the development of long-coated breeds.

Points of Comparison
Wild cats compared

EUROPEAN WILDCAT	AFRICAN WILDCAT
• Found in mainland Europe	• Found mainly in Africa
• Dark tabby	• Light-colored, with tabby rings
• Black striped tail	• Docile and sociable
• Heavy-bodied	• Long, thin tail with black tip
• Fierce and reclusive	• Lean-bodied
• Avoids human contact	• Seeks out human settlement
• Untameable.	• Tameable.

In Britain today, European wildcats have plummeted in numbers. They were common across most of the country up until the late 1500s, but woodland clearance and hunting have gradually led to their extinction except in remote areas of Scotland. Shy and secretive by nature, wildcats are rarely seen. If cornered, however, they can prove exceedingly aggressive—even a large fox might be driven away by a queen fiercely defending her kittens.

Flexible felines

The adaptability of wildcats, which has served their domestic counterparts so well, can be seen from the different habitats in which

The striking pattern of the leopard cat can be clearly seen. This cat is widespread in Asia.

they live. These range from bleak northern heather-clad moors, where rocky outcrops offer the only protection from the weather, to the warm shores of the Mediterranean, where they live in areas of forest. Wildcats also eat a wide range of foodstuffs—they prefer to prey on small mammals and birds, but will eat insects, vegetation, and even olives when other food is in short supply.

Bengal cats have become immensely popular over recent years, since their creation in the 1960s.

Crossbreeding

Strangely, no other wild cats have played a major role in the development of domestic cats. During the 19th century, classes for hybrids were common at cat shows, and a number have been recorded. It is possible that, centuries ago, cross-breeding between domestic cats and a little-known Asiatic wildcat, called Pallas's cat (*Felis manul*), led to the introduction of the longhaired characteristic of breeds such as the Turkish Angora. Only in the case of the Bengal has another wildcat been involved in creating a domestic breed. These cats were created from a pairing between a non-pedigree tom and a female Asian leopard cat (*Felis bengalus*).

domestication
of the cat

Domestication is believed to have begun in Egypt, more than 5,000 years ago. Archeological remains from this period portray cats alongside people, and show that one cat is even wearing a collar. These early domestic cats were not greatly different from their wild relatives, displaying obvious tabby markings.

The domestication of the African wildcat (*Felis lybica*) probably began by chance when cats were attracted to human settlements by easy prey of mice and rats around stores of grain. People soon saw the advantage of having cats around to destroy the vermin that ate their livelihood. Before long, cats were actively encouraged onto farms, and the taming of the wildcat would have begun.

The African wildcat is quite similar to its domestic relative, displaying the same tabby markings.

Cats in Egyptian culture

Soon cats became important in Egyptian culture as well, in the guise of the feline goddess variously known as Basht, Bastet, and Pasht. The goddess was portrayed as having a cat's head and a woman's body. She represented fertility and regeneration; and in the city of Bubastis, her springtime festival would be attended by up to 700,000 cult followers.

Cats may well have been sacrificed to the goddess. However, as many as 100,000 cats were buried in ceremonies here, so it was clear that they were being widely kept and bred. But despite this grisly type of ritual, there was a lot of genuine affection for cats as companions, with households going into a period of mourning when their pet cat died.

Beyond Egypt

For a long time it was illegal to export cats from Egypt, but gradually

The Egyptian feline goddess Basht, with the head of a cat and the figure of a person.

Egyptian cats

The first evidence of domestic cats was found in Egypt.
• The African wildcat (*Felis lybica*) was the most common type.
• The Jungle cat (*Felis chaus*) was also found, but is unlikely to be related to modern cats.

Ships' cats have always been popular at sea with sailors. However, sometimes they inflicted great damage on native wildlife when abandoned on remote islands.

Japanese Bobtail, is seen as a potent symbol of luck even today.

Neither the Greeks nor the Romans shared the Egyptians' affinity with cats. This is possibly because they had come to rely on ferrets as a means of controlling vermin. Yet cats did spread farther north in Europe thanks to Roman influence, and they traveled from here around the globe.

Cats in America and Australia

The first domestic cats taken to the New World were on board Columbus's ships, and many others followed. Their value soared as a means of controlling vermin on farmsteads and in towns during the 1800s, as settlement spread westward across the American continent. Breeds such as the Maine Coon trace their origins back to this period in history. Meanwhile, cats were introduced to Australia in the late 1700s. Again, they were kept on ships as a means of controlling rats, but their company was probably also appreciated by the sailors to break up the monotony of long voyages.

they spread around the Mediterranean and farther east, into China where they became established between 2000 B.C.E and 400 C.E. Cats were highly prized in Asia, not just for their hunting abilities. They were taken to Japan, where they helped to control the mice that were overrunning the country. The native breed of cat that developed there, the

The Maine Coon cat has a thick shaggy coat and a long thick tail. It was originally tabby in color. This breed developed outdoors with little interference from cat breeders. Today it is a robust breed that is bred in a variety of colors.

Cat fancy
and selective breeding

In the 1800s, there was a surge of interest in the selective breeding of plants and animals. Specialist societies boomed, and there was strong competition at the numerous exhibitions that were held to display the ever-increasing range of breeders' creations. Cats became part of this trend, and this led to the staging of the first major cat show in 1871 at Crystal Palace, London, England. It drew 165 entrants, mainly British shorthairs and Persian longhairs. A few years later, in 1887, the National Cat Club was founded.

The Maine Coon has recently become a popular breed for showing again.

Cats on show

In North America, show classes for cats were originally included as part of major agricultural fairs, predating those held in Europe. At first, the native Maine Coon breed was one of the only entrants. But once cat shows started to become city-based during the 1890s, and more

Some of the entries for an early cat show held at Crystal Palace, London, England. They are drawn by the famous illustrator and cat-lover, Louis Wain, who became president of the National Cat Club.

exotic breeds such as the Persian Longhair were brought over from Europe, the Maine Coon fell from favor and was considered little more than a farm cat. It was not until the 1980s that the Maine Coon became popular once again in the United States, and then gained wide acceptance internationally.

Essential Facts
Bengal cat

• Derives from the crossbreeding of domestic cats with Asiatic leopard cats.

• Semiwild in appearance and are varied colors including golden and snow leopard.

• To maintain the "wildcat" characteristic breeders continue to breed using Asiatic cats.

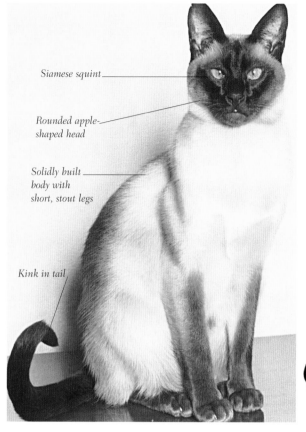
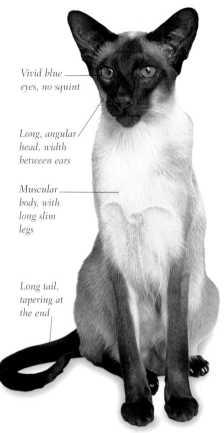

Siamese squint

Rounded apple-shaped head

Solidly built body with short, stout legs

Kink in tail

Vivid blue eyes, no squint

Long, angular head, width between ears

Muscular body, with long slim legs

Long tail, tapering at the end

The traditional "old type" Siamese (above left) has undergone a revival in popularity over recent years, especially in the United States. It is shown here alongside a modern example of the breed (above right).

Today, almost one hundred distinct breeds of cat have been created worldwide, although not all of these are wellknown, or even recognized for show purposes. Lots of factors can affect the popularity of a breed. Thankfully, since genetic weaknesses are not nearly such a problem as they are in dogs, health concerns are not a major worry in most cases.

Wild revival

Breeds that display markings similar to those of their wild relatives are becoming particularly popular at present. The Bengal is a typical example of this, and is also the only breed of recent origin descended partly from a wildcat. Others whose patterning is based on that of wild relatives include the Ocicat and the California Spangled cat. These cats have been created by careful breeding programs involving pure domestic cats.

Keeping in shape

The appearance of well-established breeds, such as the Siamese, has now changed considerably

through careful breeding. Since it was first seen in Europe in the 1880s, the Siamese has become much more elegant in profile and the shape of its head has been totally transformed. When viewed from the front it can be seen that the rounded outline has changed to an angular shape. Breeders are also now recreating the original Siamese—known in North America as apple-headed Siamese.

Meeting the breed standard

Breeders are aware that exhibition cats should be as similar as possible to the features laid down in the breed standard. The standard sets out both the desirable type or physical appearance of the cats as well as its coloration and markings. When a class of cats is being assessed at a show, the judge compares them not with each other, but against what is considered to be the breed standard.

Cat divisions

In the United States, cats are divided into two groups:
• Longhairs • Shorthairs

In Britain, traditionally cats are divided into seven groups:
• Longhair • Semi-longhair
• British Shorthair
• foreign • Burmese
• Oriental • Siamese

breed *development*

A cat that is distinctive and recognizable is part of a breed. A cat that has a color or patterned form within the breed is usually described as a variety. A recent trend in cat breeding has been the growth of different varieties within an existing breed. This is particularly noticeable with both the Persian Longhair and the British Shorthair. These are breeds that were found mainly at early shows; but other newer breeds, such as the Oriental, also offer great possibilities for the breeder. It is thought that around 400 different colors could be created in this breed—although many still remain hypothetical.

Mixing and matching

Breeds of European origins exist naturally in white, cream, red, blue, and black varieties, while both lilac and

The chocolate coloration of this Burmese cat is not traditionally seen in European breeds of cats, but comes from the East.

chocolate are colors traditionally associated with cats of Eastern origins. Now, however, the skill and dedication of breeders has made it possible to transfer Eastern colors into European breeds, creating new varieties such as the chocolate British Shorthair.

Above: The distinctive feature of the Turkish Van is the auburn color markings around its ears and on its tail.

Useful Information

Cat terminology

BREED

This is not a precise term but describes a group with similar physical characteristics such as body type. A breed has an ancestry of several generations.

VARIETY

A subdivision within a breed, usually distinguished by coloring or other features. A breed may have only one variety.

TYPE

The description includes the head and body features that characterize a breed, including its size and shape.

The Abyssinian is a ticked tabby. While selective breeding has removed barring from its legs, tabby markings are still visible on the tail and head. This breed is found worldwide and has become very popular.

Short, silky coat with a wave or ripple on the back and tail

Wedge-shaped head with medium-sized eyes and large ears

Selective breeding has also been applied to the patterning of the coat. This has extended the range of varieties in many cases. The Turkish Van, for example, is an ancient breed found on the shores of Lake Van in eastern Turkey. It has mainly a white body, with distinctive patterning and colored areas of fur on the head and tail only. Since this breed became wellknown internationally, breeders have sought to develop a similar pattern of markings. This is now described as Van patterning—in breeds such as the Persian Longhair.

Happy accidents

The number of breeds is still expanding. Although some of the most controversial breeds of today, such as the Sphynx, which is almost bald, and the short-legged Munchkin, arose naturally through unexpected mutations, most have been the result of deliberate breeding programs. In some cases, however, these have originated from a random, unplanned mating between two breeds. An unexpected liaison between a Chinchilla Persian and a Burmese, for example, provided the inspiration for the development of the Burmilla in the 1980s. The breeder in this case was so entranced by the appearance of the kittens that she decided to create a breed from them.

Pet cats with style

A number of other breeds have evolved from ordinary cats, notably the British and American shorthairs. However, they have both been subject to cross-breeding with Persian

The Cornish Rex was descended from a red tabby farm tom and a tortie-and-white domestic shorthair in England in 1950.

Longhairs to increase their size. Longhaired kittens that cropped up in later litters were removed from the breeding program. This approach has also been used more recently to develop the color-pointed group in the British Shorthaired category, where crossing this group with color-point longhairs (Himalayans) introduced Siamese-type patterning to these cats.

If new breeds do not attract the attention of other breeders, then the breeder is unlikely to be able to establish them. One such casualty in recent years has been the German Rex. This distinctively curly-coated breed now appears to have died out, largely because, particularly in North America, breeders have concentrated on the very similar Cornish Rex.

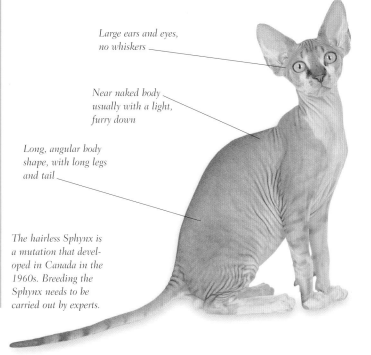

Large ears and eyes, no whiskers

Near naked body usually with a light, furry down

Long, angular body shape, with long legs and tail

The hairless Sphynx is a mutation that developed in Canada in the 1960s. Breeding the Sphynx needs to be carried out by experts.

the people–cat *relationship*

There is something undeniably mysterious about cats, which perhaps stems from their nocturnal wanderings. It is not surprising that, long after the Basht cult had died out in Egypt, these creatures of the night became linked with witchcraft and paganism, and were viewed by the Church authorities in Europe as agents of the devil. The idea that cats were witches' familiars, able to change their body shape, led to a period of savage persecution for both cats and their owners during the Middle Ages in Europe.

Famous felines

Yet it was to be the cat's hunting skills that helped to change attitudes again, especially because they

During the Middle Ages the black cat was associated with witchcraft. Some people are still superstitious about black cats as omens of good or bad luck.

provided a measure of control over rodents carrying the deadly plague-infested fleas that brought the Black Death. By the end of the 1600s, the rehabilitation of cats in society was complete, with works such as Charles Perrault's famous story *Puss in Boots* helping to restore faith in them. Other writers and artists began to feature cats in their work, and people started to view them in a different light. More recently, there have been increasingly irreverent portrayals of cats, focusing on aspects of their

Cats readily form bonds with people.

Left: Cats are easy pets to keep as part of a family.

Below: Cats fit well into the lives of individuals who may be out of the house all day.

A cat relies on its human owners for security and food, and seems to enjoy the companionship.

Cats are attracted to the warmth under a car engine, but has little sense of danger.

The appeal of cats

Over one quarter of the population of the Western world owns a cat. This may be because cats are

- independent
- inexpensive
- clean
- adaptable
- affectionate
- good companions.

A cat flap allows a cat freedom, but beware, because other cats may enter your home by this route.

personality such as their cunning, as reflected by the cartoon cat character Garfield, who has now become a popular international icon.

Popular pets

Ownership of cats has increased greatly since the late 1800s, and during the second half of the 20th century cats, for the first time, overtook dogs as the most popular pets in Britain and elsewhere. But whereas purebred dogs are more popular than crossbreeds or mongrels, there are fewer pedigree cats than ordinary cats that are descended from street cats. Nonpedigree cats usually have tabby or bicolored markings but, unlike purebred cats, their patterning is not standardized, so they are all individuals.

The rise of the cat's popularity as a pet can be explained in part by the way we live our lives today. People are now living in smaller households, and are frequently out at work all day, so owning a dog may not be practical.

A cat is much more self-sufficient and is not generally likely to upset the neighbors by making a noise, while a cat flap will allow it to wander in and out of the home at will. But there are a number of problems that stem from the popularity of cats, especially in towns and cities where there are more cats than ever before. The risk of aggressive encounters between cats is now greater. There is also an increased risk of illness and disease. Because cats are vulnerable to being injured or killed on busy roads, or being attacked by predators, many are now kept indoors.

breed
temperament

There are some marked differences in temperament between the breeds of cats. Those that have been evolved mainly as companions, such as the Persian longhair, are quite sedentary, home-loving cats, whereas those of Asian origins, such as the Siamese, are much more active, positively demanding attention. Siamese are much more lively cats by nature, both in the home and outdoors, climbing readily and often proving to be enthusiastic hunters as well, stalking and chasing birds whenever they have the opportunity.

Temperamental development

Cats that have been close to people from an early age are naturally much more friendly, and generally settle better in a family than those that have lived in relative isolation in a cattery for much of their lives.

It is only in recent years that breeders have started to develop breeds where temperament is important. The trend began with the Ragdoll—this large cat is so-called because it goes limp when lifted up and is totally relaxed when handled. More recently, the show standards for the Asian group of cats, including the Burmilla, have taken temperament into account.

Temperament has also been important in the development of the Bengal breed, because of its recent wildcat ancestry (see pages 20–21).

In the early days, some of these cats were quite shy and did not bond well with people, but now they are generally just as friendly as other breeds. Some people now breed the Bengal because of its delightful temperament. However, there may be the odd kitten that is more reserved and less friendly by nature, so it is especially important to check out the bloodline of the individual cat.

> **Winning confidence**
>
> Whatever their breed, some adult cats may be timid. To win the confidence of an adult cat
> • avoid loud or sudden noises
> • speak gently
> • provide a quiet refuge
> • let your cat come to you
> • keep visitors away at first.

While the Bengal cat is semiwild in appearance and retains a strong independence, it is an affectionate cat.

Left: Ragdolls are large, docile cats, who delight in human company and are highly affectionate.

From kitten to cat

The temperament of a cat will change as it grows older. Kittens are very inquisitive by nature, exploring their surroundings and being very playful. They may be less eager than an older cat to sit with you, preferring to chase after a small ball or clamber over a playframe indoors; but in time they will calm down.

Any initial nervousness should soon disappear, and once the cat becomes used to you, it is likely to become more relaxed in your company. It will take longer to win the confidence of an adult cat, than that of a kitten.

Neutering does have an effect on temperament, making a tomcat less aggressive, while a female is likely to become quieter and more placid. Asian breeds can be very vocal when calling to attract a mate.

Below: The Burmilla enjoys company. This breed arose from an unplanned mating between a Burmese and a Chinchilla Persian.

Above: Here a Ragdoll is seen lying totally relaxed in the arms of its owner. It is endlessly patient by nature, which makes it a good cat for a family with children.

breed
trends today

A significant modern trend is the way in which many of the newer breeds have been evolved from cats living in a semiferal state. This has resulted in their having distinctive tabby patterning. Many of the breeds originated from Africa or Asia, but some have come from other parts of the world. Here are the origins of some of the newer breeds of tabbies:

• The Singapura: This small breed of cat is one of the best-known examples of this group of tabbies who have a ticked coat. Although there is uncertainty about its origins, the ancestors of these cats are believed to have come from a colony of feral cats found in Singapore.

The Singapura is claimed to be the smallest breed of cat in the world.

Tabby variations

There are a number of variations on the classic tabby coat pattern
• mackerel • blotched
• spotted • ticked • patched.

All tabbies come in a range of colors including black, white brown, chestnut, red, silver, fawn, and cream.

OTHER NEW BREEDS
These include
• Spotted Mist • Alpaca
• York Chocolate • Nebelung
• Pudelkatzen (Poodle Cat)
• Dalles La Perm Cat
• American Lynx.

• The Wild Abyssinian: This is another variation of a tabby with a ticked coat and also comes from Singapore. However, it shares no common ancestry with the popular Abyssinian breed that came from East Africa, and is decidedly larger in size. The Wild Abyssinian still retains dark blotches and stripes on its legs and head (in Abyssinians these have been removed by selective breeding), and these markings are one of the features of particular significance to breeders.

• The Ceylonese cat (Ceylon cat): A localized population of feral cats on Sri Lanka (formerly known as Ceylon) came from the breed known as the Ceylonese or Ceylon cat in Italy. These cats are similar to the Wild Abyssinian, having ticked coats with barred markings on their legs. They were discovered by Dr. Pellegata, a veterinarian from

The Ceylonese cat was found as a feral cat in Sri Lanka by an Italian vet. A breeding program was started in 1984.

A founding group of four of these cats, known somewhat unflatteringly as "drain cats," was brought to the United States in 1975. The breed is rare and expensive, but they are hardy and friendly cats.

Above: Bobtail kittens. Their name refers to their short tails.

Right: The Sokoke Forest cat was first discovered on the edge of a forest in eastern Kenya.

Milan, who arranged for a breeding group to be sent to Italy in 1984. The traditional color, called Manila, is sandy-gold with black markings, but the Ceylonese is found in other colors as well, including cream, blue, and tortoiseshell.

• The Sokoke Forest cat: This very rare cat is one of the most exciting discoveries of recent years. It is only the second breed of African origin, following the Abyssinian, and takes its name from the area of eastern Kenya where it evolved. The origins of the Sokoke Forest cat are unknown. It may be descended from a local population of tabbies that had reverted to a feral lifestyle. Their tabby markings are quite unlike those of other tabbies. They most closely resemble cats with the blotched or classic tabby patterning, but the central, oyster-shaped blotches on the flanks are effectively broken, creating a "wood-grained" appearance. They were first recorded in Kenya in 1977. Some of these cats were sent to Denmark, where the development of the breed has continued, and there are now a few in Germany, Italy, Norway, and the USA.

• The American Bobtail: This cat is also descended from native populations of feral cats (but are not related to the American wildcat of the same name). The first example of this breed was found as a kitten near a Native American reservation in Arizona. These unusual cats have broad, round heads, large eyes and stocky bodies. They are longhaired with a short, plumy tail. The American Bobtail has a somewhat weak call, not meowing strongly like most other breeds.

the rise of the **feral cat**

Ever since cats began to be domesticated, there have been feral cats. They often live close to people's homes, but they are very wary by nature. Feral cats are difficult, if not impossible, to tame. In some cases, as with the ancestors of the Ceylonese breed, regular feeding can help to overcome their fear but often, feral cats find food entirely on their own, just like their wildcat ancestors did. They seek out quiet areas, such as in alleys, parks, abandoned buildings and rural areas where they can remain largely hidden, emerging under cover of darkness to go in search of food. They are elusive and do not trust humans.

A tough life

Feral cats are often the result of pet owners' abandonment and domestic animals find it hard to survive. The lives of feral cats are much harsher than those of their domestic relatives, and their lifespans are usually much shorter. It is estimated that a feral tomcat has a lifespan of about three or four years in the United States. When they do meet up, however, it is quite possible for feral and domestic cats to mate and, if the queen is a household pet, the kittens are generally just as friendly as those of domestic cats. When feral cats mate, however, their kittens will be wild by nature and rarely settle well in an ordinary home. The older the cats are, the more difficult rehom-

ing becomes. As a result, adult feral cats do not usually become domestic pets. Instead, they are usually trapped, neutered and released in order to keep a cat colony from disease and to stop the numbers exploding. Huge amounts of money are spent on controlling feral cats.

Above: A group of feral kittens. These cats are usually destined to have much harder and shorter lives than their domestic cousins.

Left: Fighting is common in feral cat colonies, often resulting in injuries as shown by this cat's damaged ear.

Above: Unlike these feral cats, who have gathered together, domestic cats generally do not congregate in groups, unless they have grown up together.

Feral cats

As a succesful alternative to humane euthanasia, organizations recommend
• trapping, neutering, and releasing adult cats
• rehoming tamer kittens.

A feral cat sleeping. All cats sleep a great deal to conserve energy for hunting.

Wildlife warning

The effect of feral cats in some parts of the world has proved to be devastating for the native wildlife. This problem dates back to the voyages of discovery from Europe, when ships' cats were common. Such cats were sometimes abandoned on distant shores, and feral populations grew. Feral cats, for instance, have been partly blamed for the extinction of the dodo on the island of Mauritius. In New Zealand and some of its neighboring islands, feral cats damaged wildlife that had only evolved because no predatory mammals existed there.

A small domestic population of cats can quickly multiply out of control. In 1949, five cats were taken to Marion Island, which lies nearly 1,250mi. (2000km) south of South Africa, to control mice that had invaded the weather station's foodstore. Over the next 30 years, the cats' numbers climbed

Feral cats are mainly nocturnal, emerging for food under the cover of darkness. People often leave food out for them.

to about 6,200 individuals, which were killing more than 600,000 nesting seabirds each year.

In many places today, feral cats are destroyed to safeguard the remaining population of native wildlife, but much damage has already been done. The flightless kakapo (*Strigops habroptilus*) has now become one of the rarest parrots in the world because of feral cats.

how all cats **function**

Cats are well adapted to their lifestyle. They are agile and have remarkable reflexes, which assist their hunting skills. This is due in part to their skeleton, which consists of around 244 bones, providing anchorage points for about 500 separate skeletal muscles.

Feline anatomy

• Physical characteristics: The basic shape of all cats is very similar. The head is made up of a compact skull, combined with powerful jaw muscles used to catch prey. The spinal column itself is remarkably flexible, while the long tail helps to provide additional balance when the cat is off the ground. The forelegs are powerful, ending in

Cats are agile climbers.

strong claws that help the cat to seize its prey. The hindlimbs provide the necessary thrust, allowing cheetahs to spring at record speeds in pursuit of prey, and a domestic pet to leap up a tree to escape a pursuing dog.

• Body systems: A cat has a basic circulatory system similar to our own. Arteries carry oxygenated blood from the heart, while veins take this back to the lungs to release carbon dioxide and acquire more oxygen. Normally cats breathe at somewhere between 30 and 50 times per

THE SKELETON OF THE CAT

A cat's skeleton is very strong and flexible. Its agility is made possible by the refined structure of its bones, which are moved by muscles and tendons.

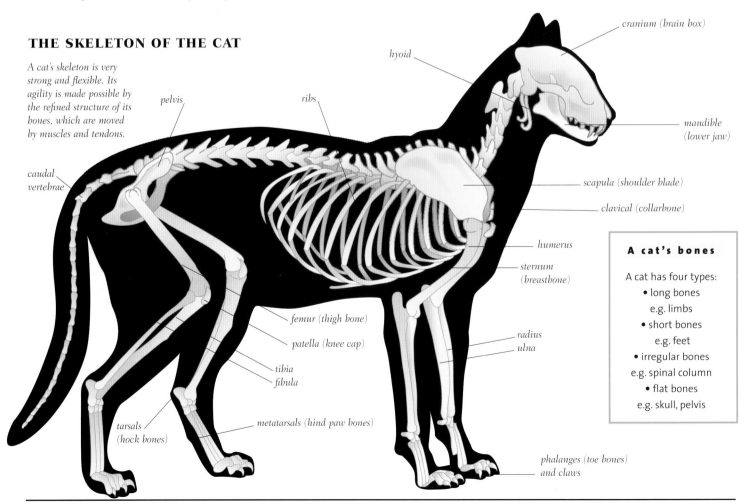

cranium (brain box)

hyoid

ribs

pelvis

mandible (lower jaw)

caudal vertebrae

scapula (shoulder blade)

clavical (collarbone)

humerus

sternum (breastbone)

femur (thigh bone)

patella (knee cap)

radius
ulna

tibia
fibula

tarsals (hock bones)

metatarsals (hind paw bones)

phalanges (toe bones) and claws

A cat's bones

A cat has four types:
• long bones
  e.g. limbs
• short bones
  e.g. feet
• irregular bones
e.g. spinal column
• flat bones
e.g. skull, pelvis

minute (about four times faster than we do). In hot weather, cats breathe at a higher rate, losing heat from their bodies through the evaporation of fluid from their lungs. This is important, because they cannot sweat effectively for this purpose—sweat glands of this type are present only between the paws. The volume of blood in the cat's body is quite small, averaging about 8 fl.oz. (250ml), which is slightly less than the contents of a can of soft drink. The heart acts as the pump for the circulatory system and is similar to a human heart, but less pointed in shape. It works about twice as fast, beating at a rate of about 120 beats per minute. This means that on average, the blood takes just 11 seconds to pass around the cat's body.

• Coat: The cat's coat helps to provide insulation against the cold. Breeds that come from northern areas of the

The Norwegian Forest cat has a weather-resistant coat, which is thicker in the winter for protection against the rain and snow.

world, such as the Norwegian Forest cat and the Siberian, both have quite dense, long coats that can repel water. They shed much of their thick hair in the late spring, when the weather becomes warmer. This can totally change the way they look because they lose the prominent ruff of longer fur surrounding the close-body fur.

Semi-longhaired breeds, such as the Turkish Angora, undergo an even more dramatic change at this time of year, so it can be hard to tell them apart from short-haired cats. They still retain the so-called brush of longer fur on their tails throughout the summer months.

Cheetahs are the fastest of all land mammals, able to sprint at speeds of about 65mph (90kph) over short distances. Their rate of acceleration outperforms any sports car.

feline eyesight

As predators, cats rely heavily on their senses to locate and catch their prey, and also help them to find their way around safely in the dark. In fact, a cat's eyes are able to produce a clear image in what our eyes see as total darkness. These senses are just as acute in domestic cats as in their wild relatives

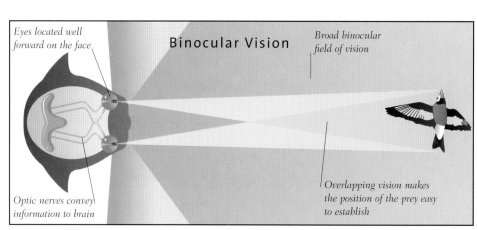

Binocular Vision

Eyes located well forward on the face

Broad binocular field of vision

Optic nerves convey information to brain

Overlapping vision makes the position of the prey easy to establish

How a cat sees in the dark

• Rods and cones: Good night vision is achieved partly by the cells on the retina at the back of the eyes where the image is formed. Cone cells are required for color vision (cats can distinguish some colors from each other), and work well in bright light; while rod cells provide monochrome images when the light level is poor. A cat has many more rods than cones, which helps to explain its excellent nighttime vision.

• Reflective layer: There is also a reflective layer at the back of each of the cat's eyes, known as the *tapetum lucidum*, which acts like a mirror, reflecting the rays of light back to the retina. This stimulates the cells and improves the quality of the image. This reflected layer is also what causes cats' eyes to glow in the dark when a light is shone directly at them.

• Eye shape: The shape of the eyes also helps the cat to see well in the dark. In species that are mainly nocturnal, the outer cornea at the front of each eye is curved. This means that when light enters the eye and passes through the lens to the retina, it tends to be concentrated in a particular area, stimulating the rods more effectively. This helps to create a sharper image, even in relative darkness.

• Pupils: The pupils expand to become circular after dark to let in as much light as possible. In bright sunlight, however, the pupils narrow down to slits, transforming the cat's appearance.

A cat's eyes are set well forward in the head and aim straight forward with a binocular vision of 120 degrees. In addition there is another 80 degrees each side, a total of 280 degrees vision. A cat's eyesight is best when objects are over 7ft. (2m) away.

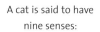

The cat's senses

A cat is said to have nine senses:
• sight • taste
• touch • smell
• hearing • temperature
• balance • place • time

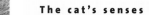

Cats have excellent nighttime vision, thanks to the structure of their eyes.

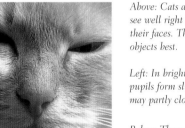

Whiskers are important in helping cats to slip through slender gaps.

Whiskers are thickened, modified hairs that connect to special nerve cells at their bases. When a cat is determining whether it can slip through a gap it can extend its whiskers to see if there is sufficient space.

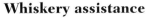

Above: Cats are not able to see well right in front of their faces. They see moving objects best.

Left: In bright light, cats' pupils form slits and they may partly close their eyes.

Below: There are whiskers located above the eyes and below the chin as well as on the muzzle.

Being able to locate the position of prey is vital when hunting, and the eyesight of cats is well adapted for this purpose. The images from both eyes overlap slightly, enabling the cat to determine very accurately its distance from its prey. Most cats have binocular vision, although it is better in some breeds of cat than others. A Siamese cat, for example, has poor binocular vision and so has to adjust its hunting technique to compensate.

Whiskery assistance

Cats also rely on sensory input from their whiskers to help them find their way around in the dark and judge gaps.

feline athleticism

A 19th century photographer named Eadweard Muybridge (1830–1904) revealed how, when walking, a cat uses first the legs on one side of the body, starting with one foreleg, followed by the corresponding hindleg, and then moves its other legs in an identical sequence. As the cat moves faster, it starts with its right foreleg, followed by its left hindleg, and once it is actually running, both hindlegs move together to give the cat its greatest propulsive thrust.

Built for speed

There are several ways in which the cat's body is adapted to enable it to run faster, with minimal effort:

• Legs: Cats generally have relatively long legs, which enable them to cover a large area of ground in a single stride. Its strong hind legs power it forward.

• Spine: The flexible vertebral column enables the body to be effectively extended.

Small wildcats such as this margay prefer to hide, but if caught in the open they will try to leap off and sprint away quickly.

A cat can stand up on its hindlegs if it is able to support the weight of its body against something solid.

• Feet: The feet assist with athleticism, as cats display a digitigrade movement so that they walk on their toes, rather than using the entire foot. This means that they can almost spring forward using just their toes, instead of raising and lowering the whole foot as they run.

• Tail: Its tail helps a cat's coordination and movement.

Rise and fall

While some species of cat, such as the cheetah (*Acinonyx jubatus*), are adapted primarily for running, others such as the margay (*Felis wiedii*), a small cat from South America, are well suited to living above the ground, in trees. Nonetheless, all cats are athletes who have the ability to climb and jump.

• Climbing: Although cats can generally climb up without too much difficulty, using their sharp claws to anchor onto

Cats can also jump well, thanks to their strong hindquarters.

Young cats can be nervous about coming down again after climbing up into a tree. Most cats find this quite difficult to master.

Left: The tail helps to provide balance when a cat is walking along a branch, or landing after jumping.

How a cat falls

When a cat falls, its organ of balance, deep within the ear can help the body land safely as follows:

- The head rotates into a horizontal position.
- The spine twists the body around to align with the head.
- The forelegs stretch to land.
- The back legs follow.
- The cat lands safely on four feet.

This means that they land on their paws, their front legs touching down just before their hindlegs and the pads absorbing much of the force of impact.

• Leaping: Leaping is a skill that requires not only precise eye coordination but also excellent balance. When a cat leaps in this way, it extends its body, jumping forward with its front legs outstretched. The legs remain in this position as the cat lands, after which the hindlegs are tucked up under the body. The prominent carpal pads at the back of each of the front feet help the cat to retain its balance, particularly if it lands on a slippery surface. The tail too plays a vital role, being extended like a counterbalance. Domestic cats have shorter tails than their wild ancestors, because they are less active.

A cat carefully assesses where it is jumping to, before taking off.

tree trunks and moving up using their well-muscled hindlimbs, most find it difficult to come down again. They are forced down backward, gripping on with their claws before turning and leaping off the trunk once they are near the ground. The margay, however, has flexible hindlimbs, with ankles able to turn through 180 degrees, helping it to retain its balance as it climbs down head-first.

• Falling: While climbing, there is always a risk that cats will lose their balance and fall, but their remarkable reflexes mean that they can swivel their bodies instantly.

hunting
and hiding

Cats are very adept predators. This is a skill that needs practise, however, so older cats are generally more talented as hunters. The basic hunting techniques are taught by the adult female to her offspring, and learning how to overcome prey forms much of the basic play behavior of young cats.

Surprise, surprise

The element of surprise plays a very important role in successful hunting, which usually takes place as follows:
1. The approach: Cats rely on stealth to get as closely as possible to their prey, before launching into a strike. A pride of lions will often fan out in the grass so some pride members can drive their prey toward others lying in wait. Domestic cats, on the other hand, being solitary by nature, will use whatever cover is available, to hide from their prey

When stalking, a cat tries to get as close to its quarry as possible, flattening its body to remain hidden.

as they approach, dropping down low on their legs as they advance, with their tails kept low.
2. The pounce: Cats will then frequently pounce on their prey. A bird may collide with the cat's body and be knocked over, making it easier to catch. Lightning reflexes are required at this stage, to grab and overpower the unfortunate creature, with the cat using both its sharp claws and the teeth at the front of its mouth for this purpose.
3. The kill: Prey is usually killed by inflicting a fatal neck bite using the long, pointed canine teeth at the corners of the cat's mouth.

Claws

A cat's claws are kept sharp by regular scratching sessions, often on a tree or stump outdoors. The resulting marks also act as a territorial indicator to other cats in the neighborhood.

This cat is fully alert, with its ears pointing forward, listening for sounds that could reveal the presence of prey nearby.

*Cats may hide both
to escape detection
themselves and also
in the hope of catch-
ing passing prey
unawares.*

A cat as a hunter

A cat is ideally suited
as a predator
because it has
• sensitive whiskers to
feel in the dark
• strong back legs
used to pounce
• front claws that
grasp and hold prey
• canines that can kill
• a rough tongue that strips
meat from bone.

The sweat glands between the toes leave a scent behind to mark territory as well. Normally the claws of domestic cats are kept retracted, largely out of sight, by means of ligaments. A similar arrangement is seen in most other wildcats as well, with the notable exception of the cheetah, whose claws are not drawn back. This helps the cheetah to maintain its balance as it pursues its prey at high speed.

*Domestic cats
instinctively
seek small prey
such as rodents,
frogs, or birds,
which can be
killed easily and
swallowed
whole.*

Teeth

Once prey has been caught and killed, the teeth at the back of the mouth prepare the food ready for swallowing.

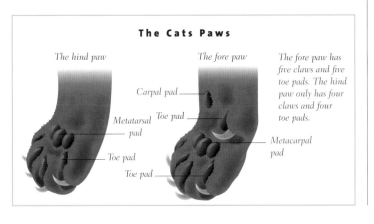

The Cats Paws

The hind paw

The fore paw

*The fore paw has
five claws and five
toe pads. The hind
paw only has four
claws and four
toe pads.*

Carpal pad

Metatarsal
pad

Toe pad

Toe pad

Toe pad

Metacarpal
pad

The premolar teeth lie behind the canines, while the molars are located at the back of the mouth. The third upper premolar and the first molar in the lower jaw are especially important at this stage. They are known as the carnassial teeth and combine together like scissors to cut through the flesh. Cats often eat a large piece of food by tilting the head to one side, so they can use these teeth. They are unable to grind up their food, since their jaws cannot move from side to side; this would weaken the stabbing power of their canine teeth.

cats
at rest

Cats, especially kittens, sleep longer than most other mammals. They sleep for up to two-thirds of the day, and adjust their sleeping period to their lifestyle. Cats that are left largely on their own during the day will spend much of this period asleep until their owners return. Cats that remain in their owner's company for much of the day will sleep for shorter periods, waking up at frequent intervals.

This not only makes the housework easier, since there will be no hairs to clean from the upholstery, but also ensures that the cushions will not be damaged by their claws.

Setting up a bed

When selecting a cat bed, look for the following features:
- It can be washed easily, with covers that are fully removable for this purpose. This can help to prevent a buildup of fleas, which are otherwise likely to cause your cat considerable irritation.
- It does not have plastic foam cushions or linings that may be dangerous if a cat chews and ingests the material.
- It is positioned out of drafts and is warm. It should be a safe retreat for the cat but within sight or sound of a family's activities.
- That it is appropriate for your cat. Older cats may favor bean bags because they can stretch out more comfortably instead of having to curl up, because their joints may not be as supple as they were.

This pattern of waking and sleeping is often described as "catnapping."

Comfort and warmth

Most cats have a favorite place in the home where they will sleep. Kittens can be encouraged from an early age to use their own bed for this purpose, rather than sleeping on an armchair or sofa.

Above: Kittens in particular will sleep for long periods.

Left: Cats do not usually sleep solidly for long periods but take catnaps.

Right: A cat on a bed adjoining a radiator where it is warm.

Above: Cats often like to sleep on beds, but this may increase the risk of your developing an allergy to them.

Left: Beware if your cat sleeps on sofas, because its claws can damage the upholstery.

• It suits your home. A suspended bed that attaches to a radiator is a popular space-saving option. This provides a cat not only with privacy, which is appreciated, but also with warmth.

Cats will inevitably seek out warm spots around the home to sleep, and may alter their sleeping posture accordingly. If they are cold they will curl their legs under the body, and their tail will come around and cover their nose and an ear in an attempt to keep themselves warm. Cats uncurl themselves and stretch out as they become warmer. Once asleep, however, a cat often displays very little awareness of its environment, and may easily end up singeing its coat by rolling too close to the fireplace or heater. An adequate fireguard is needed to prevent such accidents.

Phases of sleep

• Dozing phase: A cat begins to doze as its eyes start to close, although it will be very aware of its surroundings at this stage, waking up readily, for example, if it hears food being poured into its dish. It may even sleep sitting upright or with its head held up. The dozing phase lasts about 30 minutes. Gradually, however, if left undisturbed, the cat will fall into a deeper sleep.

• REM sleep: At this point, the cat's body may start to twitch, as it enters what is known as REM, or "rapid eyeball movement" sleep and the cat appears to be dreaming. This period of deep sleep lasts about seven minutes, during which time the cat will be difficult to rouse.

• Lighter sleep: The REM sleep is followed by lighter sleep which, like the dozing phase, also lasts about 30 minutes.

body language

Cats often communicate with each other, and with their owners, using body language. The signs are quite easy to read if you know how to interpret them, and can give you a valuable insight into your cat's mood.

Domestic cats have also evolved certain ways of attracting attention from humans that are not seen in wildcats. Look at the way in which a cat will weave its way through and around its owner's legs when it wants food! Sometimes body language is combined with more active vocal persuasion, with a cat meowing or purring at the same time to attract attention. How "talkative" your cat is can depend on its breed. Asian cats are usually vocal, whereas other breeds, notably the Russian Blue, tend to be quieter by nature.

Feline introductions

When a cat greets another cat it knows well, its tail is kept raised, pointing slightly forward. The cats approach each other directly and sniff noses.

If you want to introduce a new cat into your home it is difficult to predict whether it will get on with an existing cat. It is always much harder to bring adult cats together, compared with a pair of kittens, and an older cat may be more inclined to accept a kitten as a companion. Kittens that have been raised together in the same litter always tend to agree without problems.

Settling down

When you want to introduce cats, do not force them together, but allow them to settle at their own pace. Be sure to reinforce the position of your cat, so there will be less rivalry between them. It is important that you are not seen to make friends with the newcomer before your cat does. Usually your existing pet will be the dominant one, and this will be apparent almost at once when they meet, as shown by their body language. Introductions must be done gradually.

Cats will approach each other cautiously, especially when they are relative strangers, keeping their tails raised.

Right: Trying to introduce two cats together can be fraught with difficulty.

The Russian Blue is regarded as a quiet and docile breed.

Cats that have grown up in each other's company from kittenhood will live happily together.

Watch carefully as the cats meet each other for the first time. The meeting should always be under supervision:

• The established cat is likely to approach the newcomer, moving around to the rear end of its body and sniffing around the tail.

• The other cat will seek to lower its tail and flatten its ears in a subservient gesture before running off, which ends the risk of an aggressive encounter. The cats should meet in a place where the newcomer can slip off easily, or keep the new cat restrained to reduce the risk of conflict.

Treatment Tips
Body language

PLEASED A "chirruping" noise and head rub is a greeting from a cat to a familiar human companion.

FEARFUL OR ANGRY Tail twitches, pupils grow wider, ears flatten, fur fluffs up, claws come out, may hiss or spit.

SUBMISSIVE Rolls on back in submissive posture. But be careful because the cat can lash out with its claws if its stomach is rubbed.

AGGRESSIVE Crouched position, ears forward whiskers bristle, muscles taut, teeth bared, may hiss or spit.

RELAXED Purring, playing, washing, or sleeping. Can be submissive and affectionate toward human companions.

territorial impulse
and aggression

Wild cats occupy huge territories, which may extend over areas as large as 170 acres (70 hectares) and they lead mainly solitary lives. The size of the wildcat's territory depends on how much prey there is in the area it inhabits.

Domesticated cats are usually faced with living in areas where there are many other cats. Since they are fed rather than having to hunt, the size of their territory is less important. But mating rites are highly significant, so it is not surprising that intact tomcats in cities will fight frequently among themselves when the queens are in season. This not only makes their lives more stressful but also leaves them far more vulnerable to diseases such as the Feline AIDS virus, which can be spread by bites sustained during fights.

Above: Cats that know each other will pass without disagreement on established routes across their territories.

Right: Scratching trees and branches is a way for a cat to mark its territory, as well as keeping its claws sharp.

The cat's scent

A scent is believed to give the following messages about the individual cat.
It reveals
• its age
• its gender
• its rank
• its state of health
• when the cat was last there.
This is important for cats who share a territory.

Tomcats and danger

Tomcats range over a much wider area than queens or neutered cats, so they are also more vulnerable to being killed by traffic on the road, especially in city areas. This often happens at night, because cats can easily be temporarily blinded by the headlights of an approaching vehicle and therefore unable to react in time to the danger. As a result, the average lifespan of a typical intact tom is several years shorter than that of a neutered male.

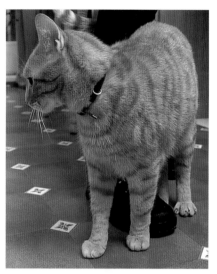

Below: Although it may seem a friendly gesture, when your cat rubs its head against your legs, it is transferring its scent, marking you as its property!

Fights can break out at any time when cats meet, especially when there is a newcomer in the area. Disagreements can be both vocal and violent.

Territories

Domestic cats have adapted to living at fairly close quarters in towns and cities. They have developed a complex network of paths crossing through each other's yards. The right of way may even change at certain times of the day. When cats do inadvertently meet, fighting rarely occurs. Instead, the individuals stop and stare at each other until one backs down allowing the other to pass, and they go their separate ways. Cats undergo a series of well-rehearsed moves before attacking each other, in the hope of causing the opponent to back down before fighting breaks out. When conflicts do occur they end quickly, with the loser running off.

There are a number of ways in which cats mark their territories to tell other cats to beware:

Marking territory

A cat patrolling its normal territory but tolerating intruders

Territory marked by urine spraying, scratch marks or scent glands

• Scent-marking: There are scent glands on a cat's head, and by rubbing against your leg or a fence, a cat will be leaving its mark, although this will not be apparent to us.

• Scratch marks: Combined with local scent-marking, claws are used to scratch posts and trees.

• Spraying: Toms in particular also use their pungent urine for this purpose. Unlike most other mammals, the penis is not located on the underside of the body, but at the rear, above the anus. This means that spraying occurs at a height matching that of the nose, so that another cat is most likely to pick up the odor even if it has rained.

A new cat in an area will have to integrate itself into the existing hierarchy because the yard around its new home might be part of another cat's territory.

reproduction
and solitary lifestyles

Living naturally on their own in the countryside means that many wildcats could find it difficult to encounter a mate. So a cat's reproductive behavior is geared to making this process as successful as possible. This means that in domestic settings where there are many cats, queens that have not been neutered will become pregnant quickly. Prospective suitors may even force their way into the home of a female through a cat flap.

The cat's reproductive cycle helps to ensure a successful mating, in spite of the cat's largely solitary lifestyles.

Luring a mate

When she is ready to mate, the female cat produces chemical messengers in her urine known as pheromones. These scent molecules carry a long way through the air and are easily detected by any tomcats in the area. When scenting in this way, cats curl the upper lip in a characteristic manner known as flehmening. They draw the air directly over a special organ called the Jacobsen's organ in the roof of the mouth that connects to the brain. The males then trace the source of the pheromones. This explains how numbers of tomcats are drawn to the place where there is a receptive female.

The female cat may rebuff her suitors at first, becoming increasingly playful, before finally mating with one or more of them.

Mating

While most female mammals have a regular ovulatory cycle, this does not apply to cats. Instead ovulation is triggered by the act of mating. It is believed that the sharp barbs present on the tip of the male's penis are important for this purpose. The result is that the female releases the eggs from her ovaries at the time when she is most likely to become pregnant, while there are male spermatozoa within her reproductive tract.

The breeding cycle

This diagram shows how the breeding cycle of the cat is triggered by communication between the brain and the reproductive organs, via chemical messengers or hormones that are carried in the bloodstream.

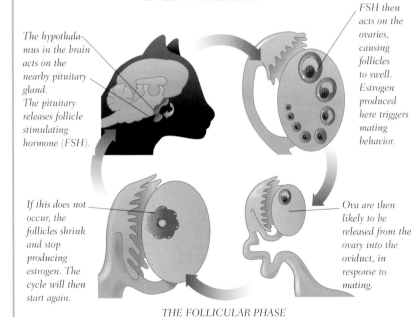

The hypothalamus in the brain acts on the nearby pituitary gland.
The pituitary releases follicle stimulating hormone (FSH).

FSH then acts on the ovaries, causing follicles to swell. Estrogen produced here triggers mating behavior.

If this does not occur, the follicles shrink and stop producing estrogen. The cycle will then start again.

Ova are then likely to be released from the ovary into the oviduct, in response to mating.

THE FOLLICULAR PHASE

Reproduction in cats

A cat's natural cycle is as follows:

PUBERTY
Usually at six to nine months

BREEDING CYCLE
Usually from January to
September

IN HEAT
Every 14–21 days in the cycle

PREGNANCY
Lasts 58–65 days

LITTER SIZE
Four to six kittens in a litter

LITTERS IN A YEAR
Maximum is about three

Summer babies

Cats will not mate throughout the year. The peak time for kittens is in early summer. This is because the cat's breeding cycle is triggered by increasing warmth and light, which occurs early in the spring in temperate areas. Pregnancy lasts for 63 days, and the first obvious indication is what is often described as "pinking up" of the

A queen with her kittens. Most female cats make excellent mothers, but if disturbed, a queen may disappear with her kittens.

queen's nipples, about three weeks after mating. Only in the latter third of pregnancy do the kittens grow significantly in size. In the case of wildcats, this means that the extra weight is less of a burden to the female when she is hunting until the final stages of her pregnancy.

the behavior of **kittens**

Kittens are more playful in nature than adult cats. Their playfulness looks very appealing to us, but it is actually a reflection of the cat's learning process. By ambushing a toy ball, for example, the kitten is continuing to develop the reflexes it would rely on to catch its prey if it had to hunt for itself.

Developing the senses

The nervous system of cats is not very effective at birth, with kittens being born blind and deaf. Their ability to use these senses develops only gradually.

• Eyes: Although a kitten's eyes will have opened by the time it is about seven days old, its binocular vision, which is vital for hunting successfully, is unlikely to be functioning fully until it is nearly three months of age.

• Hearing: Kittens are completely deaf until they are two weeks old, so they will not respond directly to sounds, although they

Older kittens are instinctively curious about the world.

Kittens are born blind and deaf, and are totally dependent on their mother until they are a few weeks old.

may appear to respond if you drop something near them. What they do detect, however, is not the noise but the air current. Even when their ear canals have opened, it will take about another two weeks before they can coordinate the direction of sound accurately.

Developing social behavior

There is a lot of evidence to show that the social behavior of pet cats depends on how much they were handled by their breeders as kittens. It is thought that early handling of kittens develops the brain and stimulates the senses. Handled kittens were found to have larger brains and became better at learning. Single or orphaned kittens grow up to be more fearful than those that have been given plenty of stimulus in the first eight weeks of their lives.

The benefits of play

- bonds kittens together
- improves fitness and ability
- mimics defense and attack
- mimics aggression
- improves hunting maneuvers
- teaches about the environment.

Left: Kittens are alert and very playful by nature, although they will also sleep for long periods. This kitten is old enough to explore its surroundings.

Below: The strong bonds that form between littermates will continue throughout their lives if the cats are not separated. From about three weeks old, kittens begin to play with each other.

Kitten coordination

The coordination of kittens is also not as good as that of adult cats, which means they are at greater risk of being injured as the result of a fall. Their natural curiosity can lead them unwittingly into danger, so it is important that in an apartment, for example, windows and balconies are adequately screened to prevent a kitten from falling.

Tree-climbing can also be a hazardous occupation for kittens because although they can climb up without too much difficulty, they often cannot find their way down again. This is why the emergency services are frequently called out to rescue cats, although often, given enough time, a young cat will find its way down unaided.

cats
running free

Cats face a number of dangers, particularly when roaming free. The greatest danger for cats is from road accidents. This is partly because cats often hide under parked cars, stalking birds that come down to feed on any remains of food that lie in the road. The cat is then likely to dart out in front of a car, aiming to catch the bird, and end up being hit. Unfortunately, cats have very little road sense. Having been involved in one accident, this does not mean that a cat will stay away from the road in the future. Part of the problem is that if a cat sees a car approaching, it will tend to carry on across the road, rather than turn back. It is then at increased risk of being hit by vehicles suddenly appearing on the other side of the road.

Feline hazards

There are other less obvious potential hazards that also have to do with vehicles. Although the risk of a cat being poisoned is generally slight, because they are very fastidious about what they eat and drink, there is a

Cats do not display any real road sense, and unfortunately many die prematurely as a result.

particular danger posed by antifreeze added to car radiators during the colder months of the year.

• Antifreeze poisoning: Cats find antifreeze appealing and drink it readily. However, it may contain an ingredient known as ethylene glycol, which will crystallize out in the kidneys as well as the brain, forming oxalic acid. The effect happens too quickly to be reversed, although immediate treatment with ethanol may be successful.

One of the difficulties for a vet faced with a cat that has rapidly become sick is the fact that it is impossible to know just where it may have wandered, or what it may have consumed.

• Metaldehyde poisoning: Metaldehyde, which used to be a major hazard to cats, is, however, now less of a threat. This chemical was often used in slug pellets and similar products, and also had a strong appeal to cats. Metaldehyde has now been largely replaced by safer products in many countries.

Various chemical products such as antifreeze can be dangerous for cats.

Symptoms of Metaldehyde poisoning are a loss of co-ordination and muscular weakness, leading to collapse and frothing around the mouth. A cat that has taken Metaldehyde may die of respiratory problems.

The cat's hunting habits can also leave it vulnerable to being poisoned, particularly in the case of cats that hunt regularly. This is because, as predators, cats are likely to accumulate poisons from their prey in their own bodies.

Right: A cat can be in danger when hunting if it catches and eats rodents that have been poisoned.

Case history

Julian and Janet Redfern were very worried about their cat, Tobias. Usually an energetic and healthy cat, over the last two or three days, Tobias had been lacking in energy and was also suffering from a slight lameness. When he started having difficulty breathing, Janet immediately took Tobias to the veterinarian. The veterinarian recognized the signs of poisoning by warfarin, an ingredient of some rat poisons. A blood test showed that the cat was suffering from anaemia caused by blood loss. Warfarin was interfering with the cat's ability to utilize Vitamin K—used to help coagulate the blood. The vet immediately started Tobias on a course of treatment including Vitamin K to reverse these signs. The veterinarian reassured the worried owners that although the poisons had accumulated in the body, if the right treatment was given soon enough it would not be too late to save Tobias.

a good relationship

2 One of the reasons that cats are popular today is that they are fairly easy to look after. But they need some attention from their owners every day. If cats are bored they may become destructive, or even wander off to another home where they feel more appreciated.

Before deciding to get a cat, therefore, it is a good idea to assess your lifestyle carefully, to make sure that you can offer a stimulating home to your new pet. It should also be remembered that cats live for 15 years or longer, so a cat would be a long-term commitment. Aside from the regular costs of feeding, and possibly cat litter, there will be vet bills for routine health care such as vaccinations and worming, and health-care insurance. Vacation times can also add to the costs of ownership if you need to book your pet into a cattery, or arrange for a housesitter to look after your cat in your absence.

an outdoor
cat

One of the important decisions you will need to take is whether your cat will be an indoor cat, or if it will be allowed to roam outdoors. In some cases, for example if you are living in a high-rise apartment, then you will have no choice, but otherwise, you will need to consider how close you are to roads and the danger from traffic. With the number of cats killed as the result of road accidents increasing each year, owners are looking again at the safest way to keep their cats.

Some cats like to take a stroll down the street but you need to think carefully about how much freedom you wish to give your cat.

However, cars are not the only danger to cats outdoors. The cost of some pure-bred cats can make them a target for would-be thieves, so they are usually kept confined for this reason. This does not necessarily mean having to keep a cat indoors all the time, for there are some options:

Dangers for outdoor cats
• roads and cars • theft • domestic refuse • predators • garden sheds • pools and ponds • traps • electric fences.

Outdoor cat homes

It is now possible to buy sectional cat homes suitable for outdoors. These consist of a run attached to a snug shelter, where the cat will be able to retreat when the weather is bad. There may be a single entry door going into the shelter, with a connecting door leading out into the run.

Above: Cats may express their frustration with being indoors by gazing out through a window and making a chatter-ing noise with their teeth.

Below: Cats will often sleep in sheds, and can get shut in as a result.

A secure carrier will allow you to move your cat safely indoors from an outdoor run.

Cats can be surprisingly fast, however, so it may also be worthwhile fitting a wire porch around the outer door. This will enable you to enter the porch and then close the outer door behind you before opening the door to the run, making sure that your cat will not be able to escape.

If it does slip out past you, then it will simply remain in the porch area, from where it can be easily placed back inside the enclosure.

Building an outdoor home

It is quite easy to build one of these outdoor cat runs yourself or adapt one to suit your circumstances (see pages 116–17). However, if you prefer, you can buy a unit of this type from specialist manufacturers who advertise in the various cat magazines. Once ordered, they will arrange delivery of the cat run to your door in most cases, and may even erect the unit on site for you if required.

The advantages

The advantage of having a run of this type, besides keeping your pet safe, is that it enables the cat to play and climb, and experience life outdoors. Many owners transfer the cat here during the daytime before leaving for work, and then bring their pet indoors again when they return home later in the day.

Choosing a Type
Indoor cats

Some cats are much better suited to indoor living than the outdoor life.

THE SPHYNX

The Sphynx is essentially an indoor cat. It has almost no fur and so no protection from cold weather. It also needs to be kept out of the sun because it burns easily. This cat is most suitable for one-pet households.

REX BREEDS

Rex breeds will also thrive in the home, not just because of their relatively sparse fur, but because of their strong personalities. They are usually intelligent, playful, and affectionate cats to have in the home.

The curly-coated Devon Rex is friendly and extrovert. This breed likes to live indoors in the warm because of its thin coat.

Clearly, it can be important to have an electricity supply outdoors, not just for lighting but also for providing heat if the weather turns cold. In this case you need to ensure that all cabling is kept well out of the cat's reach.

A secure carrier is also needed for carrying the cat back and forth between the cat run and the house.

what type of cat
is right for you?

Although nonpedigree cats are far more common than pure-bred cats, this is just one of the choices that you will make when deciding which cat is right for you.

• Should I buy a pedigree? A pedigree cat is more expensive than a nonpedigree cat. The cost may depend on how common the breed is and the type of kittens on offer. If you are seeking a particularly unusual breed or a kitten of specific color, then you may have to be patient and wait for one to become available. On the other hand, nonpedigree cats can make very handsome and loving pets and are less expensive to buy.

• What about showing my cat? You must decide whether you will want to exhibit a pedigree cat. This can develop into a very interesting hobby, but it may prove quite expensive and you are unlikely to recoup your costs.

Cats generally settle well in a new home, but some can be more nervous than others, depending on their background.

A longhaired cat (left) needs considerably more help with grooming than a shorthair. A cat has only its tongue to groom itself.

If you don't want to show your cat, then a breeder may be able to supply one with minor faults, such as flawed markings for example. Kittens like these are called "pet-quality" kittens. They will be less costly than their littermates, who are judged to have good exhibition potential.

• What about temperament? Be sure that the temperament of the breed you are interested in will fit in with you and your family. There can be some marked differences between breeds in this respect. Certain breeds are much more extrovert than others, and some are more vocal as well. There are plenty of reference books available that describe the temperaments of different pedigree cats.

• What about size? Unlike dogs, cat breeds are all of similar size ranging from the Singapura, which weighs less than 6lb. (2.7kg) up to the Maine Coone, which typically weighs around 18lb. (8kg) There is little difference in size between a male or female cat, although male cats grow slightly bigger than females.

Above: Grooming is not just for the cat's benefit. Less hair will be shed around the home.

Below: Tangles show more grooming is required.

Siamese rank among the most widely kept of purebred cats, but they have very demanding personalities.

• Should I buy a longhair or a shorthair? Whether you are attracted to a nonpedigree or a specific breed, you should consider coat length, because this will affect the amount of grooming that the cat will need. Longhairs will need to be groomed every day to prevent their coats from becoming matted (also see pages 76–77), but a short-haired cat needs only occasional grooming to remove dead hair from its body.

Maine Coons have become very popular with pet-owners over recent years, as well as on the show scene.

• What about health aspects? The natural lifespan of the various breeds and nonpedigrees is fairly similar and your cat may live up to about 20 years old. Purebred cats are generally not as vulnerable to congenital or inherited defects as dogs. When a problem crops up it is not life-threatening. Siamese cats, for example, can be vulnerable to kinked tails although this is less common today (see page 21). More serious than this are the heart defects sometimes encountered in Asian bloodlines. A vet will normally give a kitten a check-up as part of a pre-vaccination routine, so any such problems should be detected at this stage, and can be drawn immediately to the breeder's attention.

Choosing a Type
Smallest and largest

SINGAPURA	MAINE COON
• 6lb. (2.7kg) or less	• 18lb. (8kg) or less
• Short ticked coat	• Dense rugged coat
• Small body, large ears	• Large body, large ears
• Small paws	• Long thick tail
• Stocky, muscular	• Muscular, strong legs
• Hardy and robust	• Confident, outdoor
• Friendly and inquisitive.	• Active, fun, even-tempered.

getting
a cat

Many people seeking a pet cat prefer to start with a kitten around 12 weeks of age, but there is no reason why you cannot choose an older cat. There are in fact several ways in which this is better. An older cat is already likely to be used to living in a home and should prove less destructive than a kitten. It may well have been neutered, saving the cost of surgery. There are always a large number of adult cats in need of good homes, whereas kittens are not available throughout the year.

> **Getting a cat**
>
> You can get a cat
> • from people you know
> • from reputable breeders
> • from an animal shelter
> • from a vet's recommendation.

These kittens will all be looking for good homes. Color and character may influence a prospective owner's choice of pet. This is usually more important than gender.

It is important to try and discover as much as possible about an older cat, especially its age, because this could influence your choice of which pet to buy.

Sexing cats

The gender of the cat is significant if you are hoping to breed from your cat. Sexing kittens is harder than in the case of mature cats, partly because male cats do not have an external penis, nor will the testes be clearly apparent in young kittens. But by comparing the sexes with one another it is fairly easy to tell males from females. The space between the penile opening and the anus below is greater in the case of young toms than in queens. This is where the testes will later develop.

It is fairly easy to identify neutered toms, but it can be much harder to see whether a queen has been spayed. You may be able to feel the underlying scar tissue, however, as

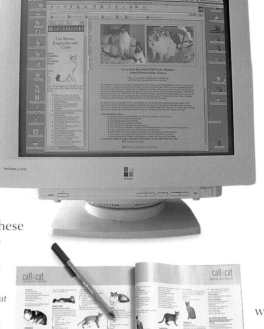

a slight raised ridge on the flank on the left side of the body, or on the underside in the midline. Many male cats, including nonpedigrees, develop big jowls when they mature. These are fleshy swellings around the sides of the face, like a double chin. A male cat neutered before maturity will not develop jowls.

Internet websites now provide a good way of tracking down breed organizations and breeders, but it is not the only way to find a cat.

Where to find a cat

If you are seeking a pedigree cat, then you will almost certainly need to track down a breeder.

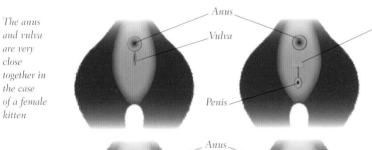

Specialist cat magazines list breeders with kittens looking for new homes.

You may be able to do this via the advertisement columns of cat magazines, or registration bodies. The Internet can also prove to be a valuable starting point for a search, with increasing numbers of breeders now having their catteries on their own home pages, illustrated with photographs of their cats. Visiting shows is an ideal way to see breeds that interest you, and have the opportunity to meet and talk to breeders. Information about events such as shows can also be found in cat magazines.

It is much easier to locate a nonpedigree kitten, since litters are commonly advertised in local papers, or your veterinarian may know of a litter seeking homes.

You may also consider getting a cat from an animal shelter or organization that has rescued cats and kittens from the street. They are spayed or neutered and then put up for adoptions after the necessary health checks and immunizations have taken place. There are many such shelters in each state, all with pets in need of a good home. Animal shelters often find it impossible to place domestic kittens and cats by the sheer volume of animals that are rescued from the streets.

Sexing cats

It is harder to sex kittens than adult cats.
Remember that neutered males will not have testes.

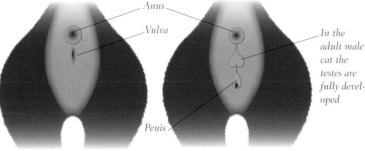

The anus and vulva are very close together in the case of a female kitten

Anus

Vulva

The developing testes lie between the anus and the penis (not external) in a male kitten

Penis

There is very little change in the case of an older female cat

Anus

Vulva

In the adult male cat the testes are fully developed

Penis

coming home
and settling in

Cats generally do not enjoy traveling in a car. If they become upset in these surroundings, they can become a serious liability if not properly confined.

Best carriers

One of the best options for transporting a cat or kitten is one of the modern plastic or acrylic carriers. These have spacer bars around the side to prevent any risk of the air-holes becoming blocked, and handscrews to allow the upper and lower parts of the unit to be separated for ease of cleaning. If you do not have an appropriate carrier, be aware of some of the common problems of transporting a cat or bringing a new kitten home in a car:

• On a lap: Keeping a cat sitting on a towel on the lap of a passenger is simply not safe, because it will be almost impossible to control if it starts lashing out with its claws.

Cat carriers

Cats must be confined for car travel. Here are some carriers

CARDBOARD CARRIER
Lightweight, economical, more suitable for kittens than cats.

WICKER CARRIER
Traditional carriers may be hard to clean.

PLASTIC OR ACRYLIC CARRIER
Easy to clean and disinfect.

Other carriers include wire carriers, which provide good ventilation and are easy to clean.

This could easily distract the driver of the car.
• In a cardboard carrier: A cardboard carrier is a typical way of transporting a kitten as it is lightweight and economical. But take care that the kitten does not push its way

Regular deworming is vital, especially for kittens and cats that hunt regularly.

out of a box where the flaps are folded over. Trying to restrain it under these circumstances while driving will be almost impossible. The base of a cardboard carrier can become saturated by the kitten's urine. This means it could fall apart it is lifted. It is always a good idea to line the interior with a thick layer of newspaper, and support the carrier underneath when picking it up.

Getting a kitten home

Try to have everything prepared and ready at home when you bring back your kitten, so it will not need to be left in its box longer than is necessary. A pen where the young cat can be confined can be useful, to prevent it from running out when a door is open. There should be food and water bowls, plus a litter pan. The litter tray is essential since young kittens cannot be allowed out until after they have completed their course of injections, and adult cats will need to be confined in the home for at least a two weeks to help them get used to their new environment and prevent them from straying off and disappearing.

Left: A young kitten will be eager to explore its new environment, but should not be allowed outdoors until it has completed its vaccinations.

Early days

You are most likely to have problems with a new cat in the early days while it is becoming settled in its new surroundings. The change of a move can be enough to cause a digestive upset, which can be serious in a kitten, because diarrhea leads to rapid dehydration. If this happens, you will need to seek veterinary advice.

Remember the following points:

• Keeping the kitten to the same diet minimizes the risk of a digestive upset, so make sure that you have the full details of the kitten's diet before you take your kitten home. Make dietary changes gradually, mixing the new food in increasing quantities with the cat's existing food.

Right: Most kittens become accustomed to using a litter tray by the time they are weaned.

• Remember to keep up the vaccinations that are required for your kitten, every two weeks. These are very important to safeguard a kitten's health, as is regular worming. Your veterinarian will advise you on the best way of doing this.

establishing **ground rules**

Bonding with a kitten is not difficult. In the early stages, it is very important to spend time with your new pet, so that you can establish the sort of ground rules that will last throughout the cat's lifetime with you.

Coming when called

• Your cat should learn its name, so that it comes when it is called. When your cat responds to its name, always give it a reward. It will then be much easier to persuade your cat to return to you once it starts to venture farther afield out in the yard.

• Always praise the cat and make a fuss of it when it responds well in any learning situation.

Walking the cat

While it is not possible to train cats to the same extent as dogs, they can get used to walking on a harness and leash as long as you begin this process in kittenhood. Certain breeds, such as the Siamese, seem to respond more readily to this method of exercise than others. You are likely to find at first that the cat responds by rolling over onto its back and starts to claw at the leash, thinking this is some type of game. If the cat is very excitable, it may be better to play for a period before starting a training session of this type. When leash training:

• Keep sessions fairly short, so your cat does not become bored.

• At first, allow the cat just to wear the harness, so it gets used to it without being restrained by the leash.

• Never use a collar in place of a harness, because if the cat becomes upset, it could injure its neck. The harness serves to distribute the weight more evenly than a collar.

Siamese respond well to lead training.

Firm but gentle

A vital lesson that needs to be taught to a pet cat at an early stage in life is that having its mouth opened is not a painful procedure. This will make caring for your cat much easier in later life, when it comes to checking its teeth, for example, or giving tablets. It is a very simple process, but adult cats that are unused to the experience resent it greatly and may resort to scratching, struggling and biting.

It is best to provide a kitten with its own bed so it does not start sleeping on chairs.

Above: It is possible to train a cat to walk on a harness and leash, but watch out for dogs if you venture into a street or park.

Left: Cats often acquire different behaviors as a result of reinforcement from their owners. A cat may learn that by standing up or begging, it can expect a reward, and so behaves more often in this way.

Opening the mouth

1. Start with the kitten sitting down, and gently take hold of its head, placing your left hand (if you are right-handed) over its face, across the nose.

2. Lift the head up, and then with your left hand, gently pry down the lower jaw.

3. When giving a tablet, place this as far back in the mouth as possible and hold the jaws shut for a few moments. This, combined with tickling your kitten under the throat, will encourage it to swallow the tablet rather than spitting it out.

In emergencies, it is possible to buy pill dispensers that release a pill in the cat's mouth by means of a plunger mechanism.

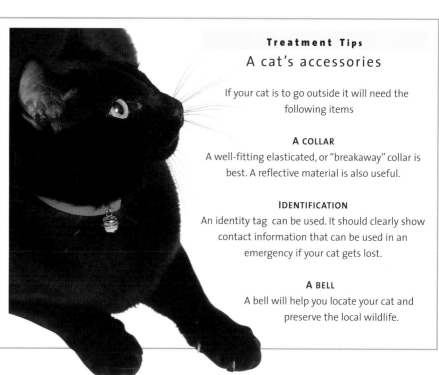

Treatment Tips
A cat's accessories

If your cat is to go outside it will need the following items

A COLLAR
A well-fitting elasticated, or "breakaway" collar is best. A reflective material is also useful.

IDENTIFICATION
An identity tag can be used. It should clearly show contact information that can be used in an emergency if your cat gets lost.

A BELL
A bell will help you locate your cat and preserve the local wildlife.

establishing a **routine**

Cats, and kittens especially, soon adapt to a new routine. It is best to stick as closely as possible to the feeding times that your pet was used to at its previous home. This will help it to settle in without problems. Always remember that after eating, a kitten is likely to want to relieve itself, so it is important to keep the litter pan within easy reach. You need to ensure that the litter pan is cleaned regularly after use, not just for hygiene, but also because cats will tend not to use a pan that has been previously soiled.

Safety first

Rather than discarding all the litter, you may be able to use a scoop to remove soiled areas, and simply top it up as required. However, you should empty the pan completely and wash it thoroughly at least once a week, using a

A cat is more likely to use its litter pan after a meal, so be prepared to clean this accordingly. Cats will actually go elsewhere rather than use a litter pan that has already been soiled.

suitable disinfectant—these are widely available in pet stores. Follow the instructions for use carefully, washing the pan off as thoroughly as possible first, because the action of disinfectants is often inhibited by the presence of organic matter.

Gloves should be worn, especially by pregnant women, when cleaning a litter pan because of the slight risk of acquiring the microscopic parasites known as *Toxoplasma gonadii*, which is the cause of the disease known as toxoplasmosis. This is a zoonosis, meaning that it can be spread from cats to people. Although generally this parasite causes little harm to people, it can cross the placenta and harm the unborn child, resulting in a possible miscarriage. It is possible to screen cats for this parasite using fecal samples.

Try to feed cats at regular times, rather than leaving them with food constantly available since this may result in overeating and lead to obesity.

with the kitten beforehand, so that it will be tired and, hopefully, will soon curl up and go to sleep while you are out. Once you come back, spend some time playing with the kitten and making a fuss of it, so that before long it will realize that it has nothing to fear from your absences.

Roaming free?

It is not a good idea to allow a kitten to roam freely about the house while you are out, and even with an older cat this is not always a good idea. Kittens especially can end up in danger—they may brush against a sharp cactus in a pot on a windowsill, for example, and end up with spines embedded in their coats, or perhaps knock over and break a valuable ornament.

> **Routines**
>
> You need to establish routines for your cat in the following areas
> • feeding time • grooming
> • playtime • bedtime.

Home alone

When you first leave your new pet at home on its own, try not to go out for more than an hour or so, especially if you have a kitten. A kitten will not be used to being on its own, having previously had the companionship of its littermates, as well as its mother. It is a good idea to play

Above: Cats, especially kittens, can become bored and may end up in trouble around the home and could hurt themselves.

Playing with your cat will help to establish a bond between you and may help your cat to settle when you go out. Choose toys that are safe for this purpose.

letting your kitten out

It is not safe to let a kitten out into your yard until after it has completed its course of vaccinations at over three months old. In the case of an older cat, you need to check that it has been properly vaccinated, because it too could otherwise be at risk of acquiring potentially fatal infections such as cat flu from mixing with other cats in the neighborhood, with feral cats posing a particular risk.

Out into the wide world

Adult cats are more likely to stray when first let out, compared with kittens, especially if they previously lived in the same area. This is why it is important that adult cats are neutered. This will make them less likely to wander, especially if they are adult toms.

Keep your adult cat indoors for at least two weeks before letting it out. It will come to identify your home as its territory when wandering farther afield. When letting a kitten or an older cat out for the first time, you can do several things to make sure that they do not wander off and become lost:

• Do not allow your cat to go out for the first time after a meal, or there will be less incentive to return.

Above right: Cats will start to investigate the world outdoors once they can be let out safely.

Left: Do not allow your kittens outside until they have completed their initial course of vaccinations.

• Do allow your cat out just before a mealtime, so that it will be hungry and more willing to return indoors when you call. This method also ensures that your cat recognizes your home as the source of its food, which will also encourage it not to stray too far.

Exploring

When letting your kitten or cat out for the first time, it is best to do so fairly early in the day. It can be hard to spot a kitten that has strayed off through a gap in the fence, for

Above: A cat needs to establish itself in its new territory.

Vaccinations

Kittens need vaccinations every two to four weeks until they are at least 14 weeks of age.

Schedules may vary from state to state.
**FVRCP
(PANLEUKOPENIA,
RHINOTRACHEITIS, CALICIVIRUS,
CHLAMYDIA)
RABIES
FELINE LEUKEMIA (FeLV)
FIP
(FELINE INFECTIOUS
PERITONITIS)**

Check with your veterinarian as to type of vaccine and state regulations.

example, as darkness falls. Always go outside with your kitten first. Young kittens may be nervous as they explore their new environment. They will sniff cautiously around them, keeping their tails quite low, and pausing perhaps to look at insects such as bees or butterflies, which they may not have seen before.

Once the kitten has explored some of the area, you may want to encourage it to play with you in the yard, chasing a small ball perhaps, which will give it confidence in these new surroundings.

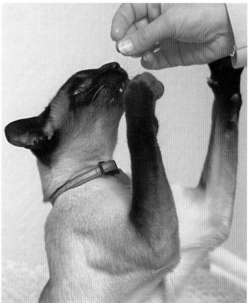

Left: Always make a fuss of your cat when it returns home. This will encourage it to return home when it is called.

Using its name

Use your kitten's name frequently, and call it to you, even though hopefully it will not disappear out of sight. Reward your cat or kitten with a suitable treat when it comes back to you. Do this with adult cats too, since they can disappear more rapidly than kittens, partly because they are more adept at jumping and partly because they may be less afraid of a new environment.

play
mates

For young cats, play is not just a form of amusement. They are practicing the vital hunting skills such as stalking, pouncing, and killing that would normally be vital to their survival. Although young cats do possess hunting instincts, these are not refined, so the skills have to be learned. This begins at an early stage. The kittens are weaned at about three weeks old when the female cat returns to her litter with live prey that they are expected to learn to kill for themselves.

Toys and games

Most domestic cats do not need to learn to kill, but still display a strong desire to play during kittenhood. Provided that their owners respond to this need, most cats will enjoy playing throughout much of their lives, often starting up a game by patting a ball across the floor to catch their owners' attention.

There is now a greater range of toys available for cats than ever, varying from simple balls to elaborate playhouses. In many cases, you need to spend time playing with your kitten, so that it becomes familiar with its toys.

Cats will often spend quite long periods each day grooming themselves. Excessive biting either indicates boredom or shows that your cat may have fleas.

Feline friends

The need to set aside an area of the home where your cat can play is especially important for house cats, which are not allowed to wander outside. Otherwise cats are likely to become bored. They may become destructive or even aggressive towards their owners. Boredom can also be reflected in ways other than being destructive—a cat may compensate in terms of its daily activities, for example it may overgroom itself by licking its fur more frequently than usual.

If you think that your cat will become bored on its own at home, it may be a good idea for it to have a companion. However, you need to introduce a new cat carefully so that the current occupier accepts the newcomer.

Mealtimes provide scope for disagreements. Even cats that know each other well should therefore be fed separately.

In these cases, it may be better to have two cats together so they can play and interact with each other to prevent boredom. If you decide that two cats would be more suitable, you need to plan very carefully at the outset to ensure that the cats are likely to be compatible.

Otherwise, you could be faced with having to rehome one of the pair if there is constant rivalry and disagreement between them.

Compatible cats

It can be easiest to start out with related cats such as littermates, who have grown up together, or a female cat and a kitten. On the other hand, problems are most likely to result when you take two adult cats, especially males, that are strangers to each other, and expect them to live harmoniously under the same roof, even if they have been neutered.

Case history

Jane was worried that her new six-month-old kitten, Flossie, was not going to get on with her four-year-old cat, Millie. She was worried that Millie would see the new cat as an intruder. Jane asked for advice. It was suggested that the cats should be separated while they settled down. Then the cats would be allowed to sniff one another between a closed door. Jane then started supervised visits between the cats. Millie was allowed to wander into the room to meet Flossie. For this first meeting, Jane kept Flossie in her carrier. But the meeting went quite well and was repeated the next day. Soon the cats were meeting each other around the house unrestrained. After a few days, each cat was sensitized to the other's scent and they had begun to get to know each other.

When cats grow up together in the same household, they are likely to be firm friends and will even groom each other.

toilet
training

Cats are naturally clean animals, and even a young kitten is likely to be using a litter pan when you acquire it. When introducing a cat of any age to the home, it is important to provide a clean litter pan while it is indoors. Otherwise the cat may simply soil on the carpet, or it may even resort to using the bathtub or the soil in a plant pot.

A cat is most likely to want to use its litter pan after a meal, so you can help your kitten to learn to become house-trained by placing it on its litter pan once it has finished eating.

To help a kitten use its litter pan:
• Pick up your kitten when it has finished eating and put it in its litter pan. To reinforce the learning you can also put a kitten in its pan after it has been sleeping or playing.
• If your kitten makes a mistake, clean the area with a safe disinfectant cleaner, and sprinkle with a little white vinegar and salt to clear the odor, or use a pet odor neutralizer. Do not scold your kitten after the event because it will not be able to relate the two incidents together.

Litter pans and litter
Cats must have easy access to the litter pan, and in the case of a small kitten you should ensure that it can climb over the sides easily. With older cats, particularly if they have painful joints, a lower-sided pan may be needed. Choose a quiet locality in the house for the litter pan, such as under a table in a conservatory, although with a young kitten, the litter pan may need to be easier to access at first. Some cats appreciate the privacy of having a hooded litter pan. This can be more pleasant for the family, but you must remember to check the box so that it can be cleaned out regularly.

This litter box provides a cat with privacy for its toilet. A cat may need to be shown how to operate the flap on this type of hooded litter box.

When filling the litter pan, pour in a thick layer. Cats will seek to cover their urine and feces, scratching the litter up with their paws.

Types of litter available
• Clay-based products: These are the traditional form of cat litter. When wet, the pieces of clay clump together. The disadvantages are that used litter can be quite heavy to carry and difficult to dispose of after use. Do not be tempted to tip this type of cat litter down the toilet, because it could end up blocking the system. Nor is it a good idea to try to recycle it, by adding it to a compost

The litter tray does not need to be filled to the top, but there should be an adequate covering of litter on the base of the tray.

Litter problems

If there are problems with your kitten or cat using the litter pan, try
• emptying the pan
more often
• cleaning it out using a
different cleaner
• getting a bigger pan
• changing the type of litter used
• moving the position of
the litter pan.

Having used the litter tray, cats will scoop up the litter in their paws to cover what they have done.

heap for example, because of the risk of introducing toxoplasma organisms to the garden. The product should be wrapped and disposed of with the household garbage.

• Wood or recycled paper: Lightweight litters made from wood or recycled paper have started to become much more popular over recent years. Wood or recycled paper can be disposed of easily once soiled by being tipped into a plastic bag (you can also obtain litter liners that double up as disposable bags for use with any type of litter), which is then sealed and put in with the household garbage. It may even be possible to burn them in some cases.

Another advantage of litters of this type is that there is very little dust associated with them. There have been concerns about the non-recyclable nature of clay-based products, which are made from raw materials extracted from the ground rather than being a recycled organic by-product.

Wood- or recycled-paper-based litter

Clay-based litter

The type of litter you use for your cat is a matter of personal choice, but light-weight litters are very popular.

handling
your kitten

If a kitten is not used to being handled, it may scratch or even bite when it is picked up. Handling is something that most kittens learn to accept from an early age, but if it feels uncomfortable, and thinks it is at risk of falling, then it will use its claws in an attempt to retain a grip. This can give you painful scratches on your skin and may even cause swelling or bleeding.

Handling kittens

It is particularly important to show children how to pick up kittens safely. Younger members of the family may face a problem with older cats too, simply because the weight of an adult cat may make it difficult to carry easily. Even a placid cat will then try to use its claws to prevent itself from falling, with the tips of the claws being sharp enough to go through clothing and inflict a painful injury beneath. Kittens are generally easier to pick up, not just because they are lighter, but also because they are less bulky.

Picking up a kitten

1. Start by scooping the young cat up from beneath, reaching under its body with your right hand (or left, if you are left-handed) and using the tips of the fingers to run along the chest to provide support.

When picking up a cat or kitten it is important to provide adequate support under the body to prevent it from struggling in your arms.

2. Your arm should provide support to the hindquarters as you lift the cat up and pull it toward your body. Talk reassuringly to your pet at this stage, to give it confidence about being picked up.

If your cat is reluctant to be caught, try to restrain it by placing your hands on each side of the neck.

Kittens should become used to being picked up by people from an early age.

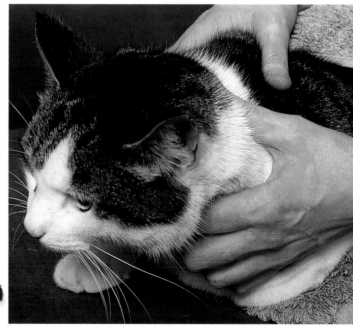

Repeat this process several times a day, so that your kitten will soon become used to being handled in this way.

Older cats

A similar approach can be adopted with older cats, but you may need to use your left hand as well, to provide greater support for the hindquarters, which are obviously heavier. As you pick the cat up, tuck its hindquarters in against your elbow. Provided that this part of the body is properly supported, then the cat is less likely to struggle. In some cases your cat may not want to be caught as it tries to slip outside through a door or a pet door. Place your left hand firmly across its shoulders, or around the front of the body. This will slow its progress, allowing you to restrain it more easily.

Distressed cats

In the case of a cat that is clearly distressed, having been badly frightened perhaps, or in pain, then the safest way to lift it up is to wrap it in a thick towel or old blanket. Place this over the cat's back and then tuck its limbs in the blanket, enveloping the cat tightly, so that it cannot escape.

Zoonoses

You are unlikely to become sick by a scratch or bite from a kitten or cat, but be aware that diseases and infections exist
• pasterella • tetanus
• scratch fever
• rabies (only in infected areas).
Always clean scratches or bites with an antiseptic solution. Consult your doctor if there is inflammation or a fever.

You may sometimes need to wrap your cat up tightly in a towel if it is distressed. This will reduce your risk of being scratched.

taking on an **older cat**

It can be very difficult to age a cat reliably once it is mature, unless its background is known. A cat's teeth may indicate whether it is still fairly young or approaching old age. The coloration of cats does not alter with age, so black cats will not turn gray around the muzzle, as occurs with dogs. If you are visiting an animal shelter in search of an older cat, however, the staff may be able to give you some background on at least some of the cats that are in need of new homes.

Rescued cats

Be guided by all the information you can gather. Bear in mind that older cats, especially those that may have been neglected, are likely to need more treatment as they grow older. Also, they may not be as easy to insure as a younger cat.

Right: Cats have fairly long lives and can live well into their teens.

Below: An older cat can be just as appealing as a kitten and in some ways is less demanding.

It is often advisable to insure your pet against future problems. However, you may need to check the small print of a selection of the policies on offer, before taking any decision as to which cat to choose.

Consider your own circumstances

• Family cat: If you have young children, find out whether the cat you are interested in has lived with a family before. A young cat that has grown up in a household alongside children will be far more amenable to having children around than an older cat. If a cat is not used to children it may be more likely to scratch or bite, not out of aggression, but because it is scared.

If you own a dog, it is best to take on a cat that is already used to dogs.

Keep a new cat indoors for at least two weeks before allowing it outside, in order to discourage it from wandering off.

• Mistreated cat: Cats that have been badly mistreated will be even harder to settle in a home, sometimes remaining very nervous, but it will be very rewarding if you can win back their confidence. Even once it is settled and happy with you, a formerly mistreated cat may still hide away when friends and visitors come to the front door.

• Scared of dogs: Dogs can also be a problem for older cats that have not grown up in their company, but simply have memories of being chased by them. If you already have a dog, try if possible to take on a cat that has previously lived alongside a dog.

Veterinary checkup

Just as with a kitten, you should arrange a veterinary checkup for an older cat soon after you have brought it home. You should attempt to find out if and when the cat was last vaccinated. This can be just as significant for older cats as it is for kittens. If you plan board your cat at some point in the future, such as when you go away on vacation, you will need to produce a valid vaccination certificate. Even so, it is not a good idea to acquire a cat (or indeed a kitten) just before going away, since it will be stressful for your new pet to be moved to another location, after just becoming familiar with your home.

> **Older cats**
>
> There are benefits to taking on an older cat. Compared to kittens older cats are
> • quieter and more placid
> • more home-oriented
> • less in need of supervision
> • less destructive
> • less prone to accidents.

Some older cats may be nervous at first in a new home, but they should soon settle into new surroundings if they find warmth, comfort, and security.

grooming
the coat

Cats spend long periods grooming themselves. If they are not brushed regularly, longhaired cats in particular can develop furballs (see page 153). The rough surface of the cat's tongue pulls loose hairs from the coat, and these can end up being swallowed and accumulate in its stomach, forming a blockage.

How grooming helps
Regular grooming of your cat is very important for good health. Not only does grooming shed unwanted hair from the coat, but it also gives an opportunity for you to
• check for parasites such as fleas and ticks
• check for skin infections such as ringworm.
Longhaired cats naturally need more regular grooming than shorthaired cats, with Persians in particular needing daily attention to their coats if they are not to become badly matted. Persians have such dense and long undercoats that they need more attention than semi-longhairs, such as the Balinese, the longhaired form of the Siamese. During the warmer months of the year, Balinese cats actually shed much of their longer fur, so they tend to look more like their shorthaired relatives at this stage, except for a long brush of fur on the tail.

Early grooming
Many longhaired breeds, such as Persians, have fairly short coats as kittens. It may take several years for the coat to develop fully over a number of successive molts.

It is very important to begin grooming quite early in a cat's life, so that it becomes used to the sensations of being groomed from an early age. However, there are significant differences in the technique that should be used when grooming a longhaired cat compared with a short-haired cat.

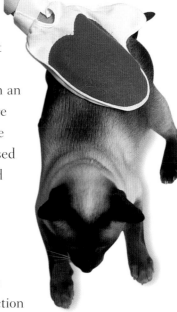

Using a cat glove to brush a shorthair. This glove has a rubber grooming pad to remove hair.

Grooming technique
• The fur of the shorthair is always groomed in the direction in which the coat lies.
• The coat of a longhair is combed vertically at first, up toward the back, after which it should be brushed back.
• The tail of the longhair also needs to be groomed in an upward direction, after which it needs to be brushed again.

Longhaired Persians need considerable coat care.

Once used to the experience, cats often appear to enjoy being brushed. Brushing can tone up the skin as well.

On both longhairs and shorthairs, take particular care grooming around the cat's head and eyes. The longer ruff of fur under the neck of a longhair should be brushed as necessary. Use natural bristles to avoid charging the coat with static electricity and causing the hairs to fly apart. During the molting period, a rubber brush can be useful

Left: Regular grooming has helped to keep this Siamese cat's coat looking glossy.

Below: This side of the glove has a soft, synthetic pad, like a chamois leather.

with shorthairs, helping to remove shed hair from the coat. As a finishing touch, especially before a show, breeders often wipe the coat of a shorthair with a chamois leather or cat glove. This helps to spread the natural oils on the hair, giving it a glossy appearance.

A pure bristle brush has short, soft bristles

Metal combs have rounded teeth with no sharp points

Grooming kit

The grooming equipment you need depends on the length of the coat of the individual cat.

SHORTHAIRED CAT
Pure bristle brush, fine-toothed comb, rubber grooming pad, chamois leather.

LONGHAIRED CAT
Wire and bristle double-sided brush, metal comb with long and short teeth, wide-toothed comb, wide flat-tail comb, blunt-edged scissors.

Left: Essential equipment needed for grooming a shorthaired cat.

feeding
and health needs

Cats are carnivores by nature, which means that they cannot live successfully on a vegetarian diet. Animal protein, in the form of meat and fish, must form the main part of a cat's food. In the wild, cats feed on rodents and birds, eating virtually the whole animal, although in the case of the birds they often use their incisor teeth to strip off feathers. Prey is swallowed head first, rather than chewed or torn into pieces, and the cat's digestive juices are able to break down the bones and benefit from the calcium present here, as well as the muscle tissue.

Dietary needs

For many years, domestic cats were fed mainly on fresh food, such as lites (pigs' lungs) and other offal. This is different from the diet of wildcats because it contains too little calcium, for example, to the extent that if calcium is not added, then the cat will suffer from a deficiency. Relying just on one type of fresh food can also lead to complications. A cat needs a balanced diet provided by commercial cat foods. Too much of one type of food (such as raw fish or raw meat) may cause vitamin deficiency or upset the balance of the body.

Tailor-made

Today it is very straightforward to give cats food that contains all the essential ingredients for their well-being. The popularity of cats as pets has grown because it is now much easier to feed them. In addition to canned foods, there are also semimoist foods, as well as a range of dry foods, which are becoming increasingly popular.

A cat needs two meals a day, whether the food is given by its owner or timed by a self-feeder.

Your cat may enjoy the occasional treat such as a meal of cooked fish, which provides it with the protein it needs.

Other pet foods

Although they may look very similar, all prepared pet foods differ in their ingredients and have been formulated to produce a balanced meal for different pets. For instance, it is not possible to maintain a cat for long in good health on canned dog food because it does not have enough protein. The nutritional needs of cats are very specific, and they need the amino acid taurine in their diet for good vision.

Milk

Milk is often regarded as a traditional part of a cat's diet. Many cats, especially breeds of Asian origin such as the Siamese, do not possess the necessary enzyme known as lactase which is required to break down the milk sugar. This means that it cannot

Nutritional needs

Animal protein (25–30%)
Fats (15–40%)
Carbohydrates (5%)
Fiber
Water
Vitamins
Minerals
Fatty acids (e.g. linolic)
Taurine
Folic acid

Left: A cat sniffs its food to check it is fresh before eating.

Tasty treats in the form of milk drops (left) and a vitamin supplement treat (right).

Crunchy sticks to chew help a cat's teeth.

Below: Commercial canned cat food is formulated to meet a cat's nutritional needs.

be absorbed into the cat's body. Lactose then ferments in the gut, causing diarrhea.

If your cat is lactose-intolerant, or if you are concerned about feeding your cat normal milk, you can use special lactose-reduced milk for cats available from supermarkets and pet stores. Milk should never be regarded as a substitute for water, which should be readily available.

Right: An enjoyable supplement for cats, containing vitamins and catnip.

feeding
routine

Cats can be very fastidious about their food, with their likes and dislikes being established early in life. It is better to introduce your kitten gradually to a range of different foods after it has been with you for a few weeks. In this way, you should have fewer difficulties with your pet later in life, for example if you need to leave it in a boarding establishment. Some cats will almost starve themselves in such surroundings, rather than eat unfamiliar food.

Types of foods

• Canned food: Although canned food is still popular, it is not without drawbacks. It will readily attract flies, which could threaten the cat's health in hot weather, and it needs to be kept refrigerated once the can is opened. Since most cats prefer warm to cold food, you should allow it to warm up before offering it to your pet, rather than using it straight from the refrigerator. Finally, cans are bulky and heavy to carry, as well as requiring plenty of storage space if you have a number of cats.

A self-feeder can keep food fresh.

The timers are set to open the lids at the required time within 48 hours. With two cats, they can be set to open at the same time.

The lid and bowl (inside) are removable for easy cleaning. An ice pack underneath the bowl keeps the food cool in the summer.

One of two compartments that can hold 1lb.(450g) of canned food each.

A cat needs drinking water available at all times, and will drink more during the hot summer months.

• Semimoist food: This food has not really grown significantly in popularity with cat owners. It looks more appealing than dry foods because of its texture—the product contains 20% more water than dry foods. Cats will eat semimoist foods quite readily, although you do not need to offer them large quantities of it. Although semimoist food

If a cat is being fed dry food, then it is likely to drink more water than on a canned diet.

As a result, manufacturers have reduced the level of magnesium in such foods and also added more salt, to encourage cats to drink more water.

Drinking

Although having access to fresh drinking water is important for all cats, it is vital for those fed on dry foods. The amount of water in such foods is just 10% compared with canned food, which consists of perhaps 80% water. Even so, not all cats drink enough to make up this difference, so it may be better to switch your cat back to a canned food in old age. An older cat is more likely to suffer from dehydration as the result of progressive kidney failure, which all cats suffer from to some extent. Dry food can be fed straight from the package and needs no special storage conditions, although it will deteriorate if not kept dry.

does not need to be kept refrigerated, the moisture will eventually dry out and it will become less appealing to the cat. Semimoist food is not recommended for use with diabetic cats, however, because sugar is used as the preservative.

• Dry food: This is now very popular among cat owners, despite initial concerns about links with Feline Urethral Syndrome (FUS). This affected male cats particularly, causing blockages in the urethra, which carries urine from the bladder out of the body. FUS was believed to be linked with the level of magnesium in such foods.

Above left: Most cats instinctively prefer to eat canned food because of its high water content.

Right: A cat's food bowl (and water bowl) must be clean, and not tainted in any way, otherwise your cat may choose to ignore what is inside it.

the method of
feeding

While the use of dry foods has revolutionized the feeding of cats in many homes, the way that many people feed their cats is very different from the way cats feed themselves in the wild. Wildcats hunt when they are hungry, and after making a kill they will often gorge themselves, digesting their meal before hunting again, so they frequently do not eat every day.

How much to feed?

The feeding instructions on packages of dry food spell out how much food a cat needs. It is always best to follow these instructions. To just keep filling up a cat's bowl can be harmful because the cat may eat too much. Cats are likely to snack on food throughout the day, particularly if they are left on their own and become bored. Before long

on this type of diet, a cat will start to become fat. If it continues to eat the same quantity of food, but has less exercise and burns off less energy, the cat will become obese, which will affect its health.

Fat cats

Surveys are finding that roughly one in three cats is now overweight. This is why it is important to feed a cat a sensible diet in the first place, providing just the recommended amount of food, rather than constant round-the-clock access to a food bowl. Early signs of obesity are not always easy to spot, because of the cat's body covering of fur, and especially so in the case of longhaired cats; but if you can no longer feel the ribcage as you pick your cat up, the chances are that the cat is already overweight.

A compartment is timed to open at your cat's feeding time.

The self-feeder can be useful if you are going to be late home in the evening and your cat expects to eat at a particular time.

Weight-reduction clinics

Veterinary clinics now run special weight-reduction clinics for cats as well as dogs, where you can obtain lifestyle advice to assist your pet in losing weight. It is important for your pet's health. Obesity is linked to a number of ailments such as diabetes mellitus. Losing weight also reduces the risks if your cat needs surgery at any stage, partly because it can be much harder to keep the sutures in place after the operation if your cat is overweight.

The coloration of Siamese cats is affected by diet and its environment. Excessive manganese darkens its points.

Obesity is becoming a more common problem in cats. It is not just a matter of overfeeding: too little exercise for housebound cats will also contribute to this problem.

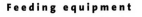

Feeding equipment

There is a variety of feeding bowls you can choose from
• Stainless steel
Longlasting and easy to clean
• Ceramic
Longlasting, easy to clean but if cracked should not be used
• Plastic
Economical, lightweight and unbreakable.

Treats and supplements

Some owners worry that their cats may not be receiving sufficient vitamins and minerals, so they offer their cats supplements and treats. However, you should avoid these unless they are prescribed by your veterinarian. Otherwise, the consequences could be harmful. Too much manganese in the diet, for example, can darken the coloration of the points of Siamese cats. Supplements can also make a cat's obesity worse.

Case history

Mrs. Jones was the owner of Bobby, a twelve-year-old black cat. She had noticed that Bobby had recently become a bit overweight. She went to the clinic about the problem the following week. The veterinarian weighed Bobby and checked his general health. The vet agreed that something needed to be done about Bobby's weight to avoid obesity affecting his health. Because Mrs. Jones lived in a top-floor apartment, she would find it difficult to increase Bobby's exercise, so instead, she would reduce Bobby's food intake. The first step would be to stop feeding Bobby table scraps, and then to reduce his main meals gradually, particularly lessening the proportion of dry food she gave to Bobby. Feeding Bobby twice a day only and taking his food away after 15 minutes would help Bobby to lose the weight he had gained.

bonding
with your cat

Your cat and you will soon evolve a routine together. This will include not just regular meals and grooming sessions but also time so that you can play together. Spending time with your cat will help you to get to know your pet better. This is valuable because you will find it easier to recognize any early symptoms of illness by a change in its behavior.

Right: Cats can be very mischievous, as shown by this individual playing under the bed.

Left: Bonding with your cat. Try to set aside some time each day for stroking your cat or playing a game.

This means that you can obtain veterinary advice and treatment without delay, which will in turn help your pet's recovery.

Telltale symptoms

Provided that their vaccinations are kept up-to-date, and they are treated as necessary against both internal and external parasites, cats are very healthy creatures and rarely get sick. However, you should look out for the following changes:

• Loss of appetite: This may indicate that your cat is sick (although in some cases, it can also mean that your cat is eating elsewhere, possibly at a neighbor's where it has found food that is more to its liking).

• Playing with food: If your cat is merely playing with its food, rather than swallowing it, this is a more likely indicator of possible health problems ranging from a painful tooth to a sore throat or ulcerated tongue, and even a hairball in the stomach or lower down the digestive tract. This is where the diagnostic skill of your veterinarian is important, to distinguish between all the

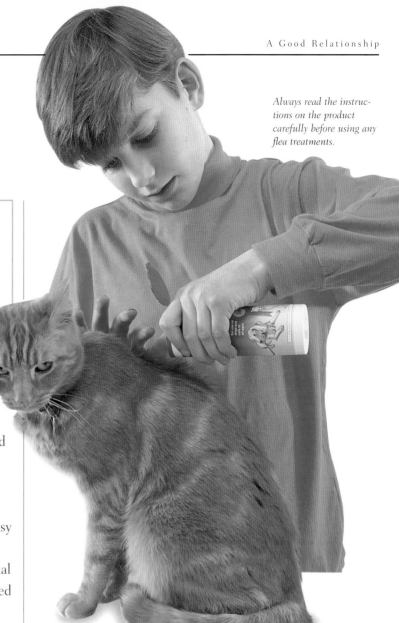

Always read the instructions on the product carefully before using any flea treatments.

Treatment Tips
Health checks

UP TO 12/14 WEEKS
Immunizations and treatments as advised by the veterinarian.
FOUR TO SIX MONTHS
Neutering in females and males.

12 MONTHS
Booster immunizations and a general health check from the veterinarian.

---

possible causes, determine the exact nature of the problem, and provide correct treatment. Even so, if you have a cat that is used to being handled by you then you may well be able to find the cause of the problem and take specific action.

The fight against fleas

The indications that a cat has a problem with fleas are easy to spot (also see pages 132–133):

• Symptoms: A cat that is scratching itself more than usual is likely to be suffering from fleas, which can be eliminated by suitable treatment. Grooming your cat's coat with a narrow-toothed flea comb will reveal the blackish specks of flea dirt, confirming the presence of these parasites. You are less likely to see the adult fleas themselves.

• Remedy: One of the latest group of products comes as a liquid that can be applied to the cat's skin. It contains IGRs or insect growth regulators that pass into the flea's body when it bites your pet, and ultimately into the flea's eggs.

Worms

Your cat is at risk of worms if it has fleas. In a young kitten this may cause
• diarrhea
• constipation
• anemia.

Seek advice if you suspect worms since it can easily be cleared with medication. An indoor cat, free of fleas, only needs occasional treatment.

IGRs have been specifically developed to prevent the fleas from completing their life cycle, so that ultimately the population will decline. In a bad infestation, however, where there are many adult fleas, you will need to resort to sprays or powders to reduce their numbers more quickly.

As you get to know your cat better you will also know when it is sick and needs proper attention.

cats and
water

Although it is popularly thought that cats dislike water, there are a number of species of wildcats, including the tiger, that venture into water regularly. Even domestic cats will often be drawn to play with a dripping faucet, trying to catch the droplets of water with their paws.

It is a myth that all cats dislike water. Tigers may swim regularly.

The cat swimmer

The Turkish Van is a breed native to Lake Van in Turkey (see pages 22–23). This local breed swims in the lake regularly, although no one is sure why they first started to do this. It has been suggested that these cats may have originally taken to the water as a means of cooling themselves in the stifling heat of a Mediterranean summer. But it is also thought they might have been acting in a similar way to the wild fishing cat (*Felis viverrina*) of southern Asia. The Turkish Van cats began to enter the water in search of fish, and then

started to venture into deeper water. Cats are good swimmers, with their legs providing powerful thrust beneath the surface and their tail acting as a rudder on the surface. Tigers have been known to travel up to 3 mi. (5km) in this way. When they emerge from the water, they simply shake their coats dry.

Bathtime

It is not usually necessary to wash cats. If their legs become muddy, it is generally better to allow the mud to dry once they return home. As soon as the mud has dried, you can simply brush it out of the coat. But occasionally a bath may be a necessity.

Right: Like this cat in the bathtub, cats can become fascinated by dripping or moving water.

Below right: Cats may even jump up or climb into a sink to drink drips from a faucet.

> ### Bathing a cat
>
> To bathe or shower
> a cat
> • have the equipment ready
> • find someone to help you
> • groom the cat first
> • clip the cat's claws
> • test the water temperature
> • work quickly
> • have towels at hand.

Showing cats

In the case of show cats, however, a bath in the period leading up to the show may be vital, especially for white and cream cats, where any staining or dirt on the coat will show clearly, spoiling the cat's chances. The bath should be given a few days before the show so that the fur will have regained its natural appearance. This applies especially to Rex breeds, whose naturally wavy coat will usually appear somewhat flattened after a bath.

If you are likely to have to bathe your cat regularly, it is a good idea to do this occasionally from an early age, so that your cat gets used to it. A baby's plastic bath basin is ideal, and you will also need a pitcher to rinse the cat.

Giving a bath

Start by filling the bath with tepid water, so that there is about 2in. (5cm) of water in the bottom.

1. Place the cat gently in the bath and start by wetting its hindquarters, moving forward up the body, keeping the head dry at this stage.

2. Gently work the shampoo into the cat's coat, and then rinse it out. Wash the head last, being careful to prevent shampoo from entering the eyes.

3. Wrap the cat in a towel, and wait until it has dried.

Cats can be quite patient about being bathed, but have everything organized first. If your cat is nervous, keep the water level low, and use a cup to pour the water gently over its coat. Use a hairdryer to dry its coat only if your cat will tolerate it.

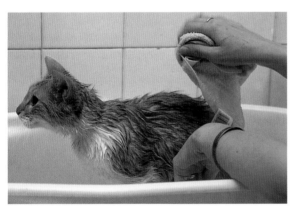
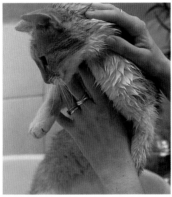

Treatment Tips
Bran bath

You can give a bran bath to shorthaired cats such as Siamese, Burmese, and Orientals to make their coats gleam.

If showing your cat, give a bran bath about two days before a show.

To give a bran bath Use about 6oz. (170g) of bran. Warm the bran in an oven first if possible.
Rub the bran into the cat's coat, rubbing against the growth of the coat.
Gently remove the bran from the coat using a brush.

the importance of **play**

The choice of toys now available for cats is larger than ever before, and ranges from small lightweight balls they can pat around with their paws, to climbing frames that can fill a large area of a room and are ideal for cats living indoors. Providing an activity center for a housebound cat means that it is less likely to become bored, and it will encourage the cat to exercise. Cats rarely play alone, and you may well have to show your pet how to use some toys in the first instance.

What to choose?

• Do not be seduced by bright packaging and stylish designs. A cat will play with a cardboard box. The robust nature of a toy is far more important, because a cat can be quite vicious toward its toys and may be quite capable of dismantling them easily with its teeth and claws.

Right: Cats have their own favorite toys, but they are more fun for the cat if you play with them too.

A cat will enjoy something as simple as a cardboard box to play with and take the occasional nap in, or to use as a place to scratch its claws.

There is no guarantee that they will be used gently, and any that are held together by sharp pieces of wire hidden inside could be dangerous to your pet.

• It is also very hazardous to choose any toy that might be swallowed and thereby creating an obstruction in the throat. The risk is probably greatest in the case of homemade toys of any kind. This point needs to be emphasized to children, who may use a small ball from one of their games to play with a kitten, which then ends up choking itself.

• Another potential danger is wool. Wool can easily wrap around the teeth and end up being swallowed. A stout piece of rope pulled across the floor is a much better option for a cat to chase after and pounce on, since it is less likely to cause damage.

This catnip mouse with a bell makes a fun toy.

Above: The squeaky noise of this toy mouse can help to attract your cat's attention.

Feline toys

Here are some ideas for inexpensive toys for a kitten or cat
- ping-pong balls
- paper grocery bag
- cardboard box
- rolls of cardboard
- stuffed cotton socks
- small ice blocks for sliding
- light from a flashlight or laser pointer.

Each cat is likely to have its own favorite toy. If you are seeking larger play areas for a housebound cat, consider the flexibility of the systems on offer. They can be expensive, although some can be expanded quite easily. You can start with the basic equipment and make additions at a later time, which will add variety for your cat.

Right: Lightweight feather toys often intrigue cats. A cat will paw at any suspended toy, sitting up on its hindquarters.

Case history

John had noticed that the herb growing in his garden seemed to have an effect on the local cats. The cats would come into his garden and sniff, nibble, and even roll on their backs in the bed of herbs. John decided to find out why cats seemed to go crazy over the herb. He found out that it was catnip (*Nepeta cataria*), a member of the mint family also known as catmint. The herb contains an oil called neptalactone, which is an active compound that causes a reaction in some cats for a short period of time. For others, the herb has no effect at all. He also discovered that the manufacturers of cat toys had incorporated the dried herb into many toys that are available for cats.

harmonious
households

If you have other pets in your household, then obviously your cat will have to integrate alongside them. Should you already own a dog, you will need to supervise meetings between your dog and cat at the outset, to ensure that there is no aggression between them. The risk is probably greatest if you are introducing a kitten into a home where there is already a large dog, not necessarily because of any desire on its part to harm your new pet, but simply because of the difference in size between them.

Feeding

It is a good idea to allow them to meet initially when the kitten is confined in its pen, making sure that your dog cannot clamber in to steal the young cat's food. They must always be fed apart, because if the dog continues to behave in this fashion it could be met with an aggressive response as the cat grows older.

When you keep both a cat and a dog, you should give them their own feeding bowls and the correct type of food.

Friends or foes?

Certain breeds of dog will settle more readily with cats than others. Generally speaking, small companion breeds are easier to keep alongside cats, because they are of similar size and do not possess strong hunting instincts, unlike hounds. Since dogs are generally social by nature, however, they are soon likely to accept a cat as a surrogate dog in the household, and if you obtain a puppy and kitten at the same time, they are likely to grow up firm friends.

Top dog?

It is even not unknown for a dog to rush outdoors to defend the cat if it is being threatened by another cat. However, if your dog starts to chase your cat, you should try to stop this before it becomes habitual. Otherwise there is a risk that your dog could injure the cat, although usually it does not take long for the cat, even a kitten, to usurp the dog's dominant role. This shift in the relationship is usually

Puppies rarely trouble cats, since a cat is quite able to control a playful puppy with a well-timed swipe of the paw. Dogs and cats should have their own spaces to sleep in.

If you have lots of pets in a home, you need to be careful about the smallest, which are the most vulnerable.

Treatment Tips

Compatible pets

- keep the feeding areas of the dog and the cat separate
- give equal attention to the dog and the cat
- feed the dog and the cat at different times of the day
- provide a dog and cat with their own sleeping arrangements
- keep the cat's litter tray away from the dog
- do not let the dog chase the cat or the cat will become defensive.

Dogs and cats can live together as part of the same family.

preceded by a swift blow across the dog's nose with its paw, but here again, aggression is not to be encouraged, because it could be that your dog ends up with an injured eye.

Out of harm's reach

Keep small pets such as rodents or birds well out of your cat's reach, preferably in a part of the home where your cat will not normally be allowed. Great care must be taken to keep the door of the room shut, especially when you go out, so that your cat is not left in the company of a small pet. Even if it does not inflict direct harm, the continued harrying by the cat in your absence may cause stress.

Small pets are even more vulnerable when out of their quarters, so always check that your cat is elsewhere and cannot come into the room before allowing your small pet out.

the purring and
roaring of cats

One of the most obvious and yet puzzling noises produced by cats is the sound of purring. This is often regarded as a sign of relaxation and general well-being, but actually cats that are in severe pain will frequently purr as well.

Domestic cats are unable to roar like their larger relatives because of a significant difference in the structure of the way in which the hyoid bones attach the larynx to the skull. These are made of cartilage in big cats, allowing greater movement, while the large chest capacity also assists in producing a louder sound.

How do cats purr?

The other puzzle about purring is that no one knows how cats make this sound, although there are two possible explanations. It is only the so-called smaller cats, including the domestic cat and its wildcat ancestors, that do purr, with larger species roaring instead.

• Explanation 1: Sound is usually produced in the voice box or larynx. It is thought that purring is the result of air passing in and out of this organ and stimulating the false vocal chords.

Small cats are unable to roar like their larger relatives.

Above: The roar of a large cat carries a long way, reinforcing its territorial claims.

This is supported by the fact that there is a distinctive gap in purring between the inspiratory and expiratory phases of the breathing cycle.

It is even possible for cats to be purring without making a sound—you can examine this yourself by placing your finger on the throat over the voice box of a cat, and feeling the vibration.

Female domestic cats can become especially vocal when seeking a mate.

When cats purr

NURSING MOTHER AND KITTENS
Kittens purr to their mother to tell her that they are feeding. She purrs in return to let them know all is well.

SICK OR INJURED CAT
Purrs to comfort itself and as a possible signal to others that it is unwell.

CONTENTED CAT
Purrs to indicate that it is in a friendly, social, nonthreatening mood toward people or other cats. A cat often purrs in expectation of food.

Even cats that are injured or ill will purr. Purring is not always a sign of contentment.

• Explanation 2: Less widely accepted today is the explanation that purring is the result of alterations in the blood-flow in the major vein known as the posterior vena cava, which returns all the blood from the hindquarters to the heart. The resulting turbulence in this vessel is said to be transmitted to the windpipe and affects the vocal chords.

Why do cats purr?
The reason for purring is equally mysterious, but it is thought that these distinctive sounds may help a mother to keep in touch with her kittens, without betraying her presence to would-be predators in the area.

Purring is not a loud sound, but it is persistent and distinctive. It could enable young cats to find their way back to their mother if they become separated, once they have become more mobile.

Calling and roaring
The other calls of cats, which can awaken the neighborhood, are the shrieks of a female cat in estrus, described as "calling." Some breeds such as Siamese are particularly vocal when calling, whereas others such as Persians are much quieter, to the extent that it may not even be obvious they are in heat.

The loud calls, often uttered at night, are used in conjunction with pheromones (see pages 46–47) to help male cats in the area to find their way to the queen. Queens only call when they are in heat, so this can be resolved by neutering or the use of hormonal preparations that can be injected into queens to stop them from calling.

care of the
teeth

The cat relies very heavily on its teeth and claws for a wide range of activities, and not just hunting. The claws, for example, are also vital for climbing and for scratching the fur, while the teeth too have an important role in grooming. It is essential to keep these areas of the body manicured for the cat's general well-being.

Teeth-brushing

There are now special kits available, containing specially designed toothbrushes and formulated toothpastes, that can be used for brushing a cat's teeth, but it is important to get your cat used to this from early in kittenhood, or it is likely to resent it. Should you not have one of these kits and want to brush your cat's teeth, never be tempted to use ordinary toothpaste, because the froth that this causes in the mouth will cause your cat considerable distress.

Instead, use some wet baking soda (sodium bicarbonate) applied on a child-size toothbrush, or wipe the teeth with a ball of absorbent cotton dipped in baking soda. This is an effective cleaner, but the task can be made much easier if you have someone else to hold the cat's mouth open. Alternatively, there are some toothpastes that cats can lick for themselves and do not involve brushing.

Dental problems

• Gum erosion: Cats do not develop cavities in their teeth, but they are very vulnerable to erosion of the gum line, caused mainly by tartar. This accumulation occurs because

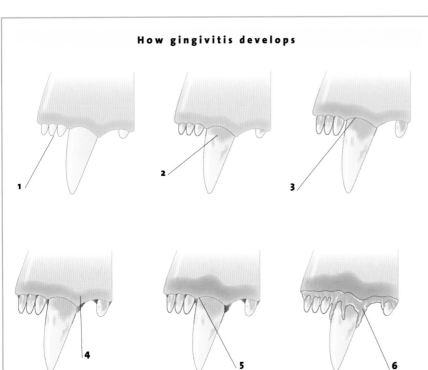

How gingivitis develops

1 *Buildup of food debris between the teeth starts primary inflammation.*

2 *Tartar and calculus (a hard mineral-based deposit) build up on the teeth.*

3 *The gum line begins to recede, leaving the teeth open to infection.*

4 *More food collects causing inflammation under the gums.*

5 *A secondary infection occurs and makes the gums appear red and swollen.*

6 *Tooth sockets loosen and there is discharge from the gums.*

Dental descaling under anesthetic removes the deposits built up on the teeth. However, viral infections can also cause the problem, so the cat should be checked for these, too. Some cats may continue to have problems with their gums and need to be kept on long-term antibiotic treatment.

Smelly breath

Halitosis in cats may be caused by
• teething • diet
• gingivitis
• abscessed tooth.

there is less regular contact with food on this area of the teeth. Feeding dry food helps to prevent a buildup of tartar, because it does not stick to the teeth as readily as wet food.

Once bacteria has become established in the food debris, gingivitis starts to occur, with the gum area becoming red and inflamed. The tartar hardens into a deposit here, and by this stage, it will need to be removed by a vet. Otherwise, the condition progressively worsens, with the erosion of the gum undermining the root of the tooth, so it becomes loose

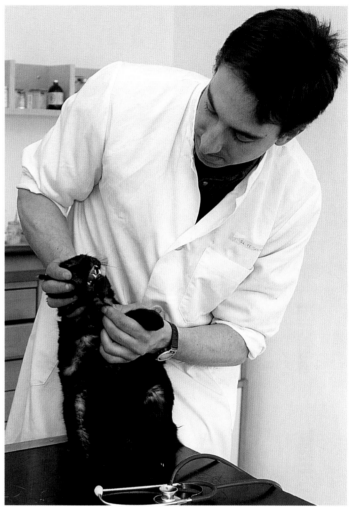

Checking inside the mouth may highlight dental or even other health problems.

Some cats are more amenable to a veterinary examination than others.

in the socket, and eating is then likely to be painful for the cat. There is also a risk of an abscess forming beneath the tooth, which can be very serious and will require the veterinarian to prescribe antibiotic treatment.

• Halitosis: Bad breath (halitosis) is a feature of more advanced dental disease, as is drooling saliva and pawing at its mouth. Be careful when attempting to open the cat's jaws, because this area will be painful and your cat may respond aggressively. Prevention by means of good dental hygiene is very important in safeguarding your cat's well-being through into old age, and this is something that needs to begin early in life.

Hunting
and wildlife

Cats that are allowed out on a regular basis will hunt and catch prey. Although the success rate of kittens will be lower than that of an adult cat at first, you may soon find that your cat brings home dead birds and rodents that it has caught in the neighborhood.

These may simply be left for you to find, with the cat making no attempt to eat them. If the unfortunate creatures are still alive, you will need to catch them and either end their lives humanely or take them to a wildlife rehabilitation center. Even if the shock of the encounter itself does not kill the bird, just a minor bite is likely to

develop into a fatal general infection. This is a result of the unpleasant bacteria naturally present within a cat's mouth. Birds frequently die several days later from such attacks, caused by deep bite wounds from the cat's canine teeth.

Wildlife warning

There is no point trying to scold a cat that hunts regularly and brings its prey home. It is simply acting as a predator. It also shows that a cat feels at home with you and wants to share its trophy with you. The number of wildlife casualties alters depending on the season of the year.

Above: Unlike lions, domestic cats do not hunt together to any extent.

Left: A cat will generally guard its quarry from another cat, even if the two cats are normally close companions.

In temperate climates, there are more casualties in the late spring and early summer, when birds are breeding. Nests containing young birds can be raided, and these newly fledged birds are much easier targets than wary adults. During the winter, the number of birds caught by cats is greater, because birds are forced out into the open in search of food and water, and are more vulnerable.

Cats like to hunt among the bushes and undergrowth.

They are likely to find small prey among the grass.

Some places have laws to protect wildlife. If you live in an area that does not protect birds, you can prevent them being ambushed by adopting certain practices:

• Site a bird feeder in an open area of the yard, away from bushes, where a cat could hide in wait. This applies also if you sprinkle food on the ground for the birds to eat.

• Place suspended feeders on thin branches that will not support the weight of a cat.

• Fit your cat with a bell, or ask for your neighbor's cat to be fitted with one, to warn wildlife that a cat is approaching. However, most cats soon adapt their hunting technique to take account of the bell. They move more slowly, keeping the head level, so the small ball within the bell does not move and make a sound.

Left: A bell attached to an elasticated collar helps to protect wildlife.

Below: Some cats are much more determined hunters of outdoor creatures than others.

Case history

The Robbins family were enthusiastic bird watchers. In the spring, birds would nest in the nesting boxes that were attached to the trees in their overgrown orchard. They were worried by their neighbor's cat, Moe, who regularly entered the orchard, lay in the long grass and tried to chase the birds. Their neighbors, Moe's owners, suggested that Moe was only acting as a natural predator. But the Robbins were worried that the young birds would be vulnerable to attack. Moe's owners agreed that Moe would wear a bell at all times on her elasticated collar to sound an alert to the birds. She would also be kept indoors at dawn, when the birds would be looking for food on the ground. The Robbins would, in turn, make the orchard less appealing to the cat by keeping the grass low and re-siting their nesting boxes away from the trees.

a safe environment

3 Your cat is a member of the family. It also needs special consideration in order to keep it safe and well in a home environment. There are many potential hazards, both inside and outside the home, that a cat may encounter, and it is important to be aware of these to safeguard your pet's welfare. The hazards may change with the seasons and can be influenced to some extent by where you live. Although it is never possible to remove risk factors entirely, you can take steps to minimize them. In this part of the book we look at how a cat is integrated into the home, and its needs at different times of its life—for instance when it is sick, pregnant, or raising kittens of its own.

welcoming
a kitten home

If you are well prepared for your kitten's arrival (also see pages 60–61), it will make it easier for the kitten to integrate itself into your house and feel at home. Ideally you will have put aside a weekend or the start of a vacation from work in order to give your pet the attention that it needs when settling in.

The basic equipment you will need for your kitten can be listed as follows:

- a bed and bedding
- a feeding dish
- a water dish
- toys
- a harness and leash
- a collar
- a litter pan
- a scratching post
- a cat carrier
- a grooming kit

Kittens will need toys to keep them amused.

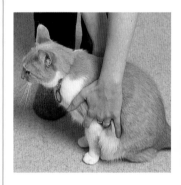

Have everything ready for your kitten when you bring it home. Make sure your kitten knows where to find its food bowl, litter tray, and bed.

Your kitten's home

Don't be surprised if when you get it home, the lively and sociable kitten you chose from a litter has turned into a nervous and timid pet. The upheaval of moving home is a very traumatic experience for a kitten who is used to being with its mother, its littermates, its former owners, and all the other things it has come to know. It can help a kitten to settle if it has something to remind it of its old surroundings, such as a familiar toy or a bed.

Some kittens adjust well to their new home, and settle in quickly. Others may look for a suitable hiding place and creep away. In both instances it is best to continue with activities as usual. The sounds of family life carrying on as normal can be quite comforting to a kitten who is frightened and unsure.

Treatment Tips
Handling your pet

When picking up a cat or kitten:

1. Place one hand under the chest, just behind the front legs.
2. Place the other hand under the rump for support. Lift into the crook of your arm.

Do not lift your kitten by the scruff of the neck since this is only suitable for very young kittens and can damage the muscles. A fully-grown cat will need the most support.

wandered out through an open door, only to find that it has just curled up to sleep in a snug place, such as under a chest or a bed. To save panics of this type, you can restrict the kitten's domain at first. It may be best to keep your kitten in one room for a few days, making sure that the windows are shut so it is not tempted to escape. After this, your kitten can explore the whole house, which should be thoroughly "cat-proofed" first (see pages 104–107). Even if you have taken on an older cat, it is still wise to follow this procedure.

Even if you have taken on an older cat it needs to feel safe, secure, and welcome in its new home, in the same way as a kitten.

It is a good idea to provide a scratching post from the start, because once your kitten has learned how to use it, it should continue to use it throughout its life.

Soon, curiosity will draw the kitten out of its hiding place and it will start to explore its new surroundings.

Exploring a home

Unless you are careful, a kitten exploring its new home can easily disappear out of sight. You may be anxious that it has

safeguarding
your home

You also need to be aware that your kitten can cause damage to your home, so you need to be careful. In the wild a cat uses its claws to catch prey, to protect its body, to climb trees and to mark its territory. In your home, your kitten uses its paws to explore and its claws to dig into things to keep a grip. Your kitten's claws will be pulled in for most of the time. However, all kittens need somewhere to scratch to sharpen their claws—as do all cats. When scratching, the outer layer of the claw falls off and is replaced by a new sharp one. This natural activity may cause damage to furniture and furnishings.

Right: You may wish to discourage your cat from damaging the furnishings with its claws.

Below: Trimming the claws every two weeks is helpful. Declawing, however is a painful surgical procedure that is allowed in the United States but not permitted in Europe.

A scratching post will give a cat somewhere to scratch its claws. You need to encourage a kitten or cat to use it.

Scratching post

This is why a scratching post is often essential. It usually consists of cord wound around a post, which the cat can scratch with its front claws. Gentle persuasion may be needed to encourage a kitten to use a scratching post.

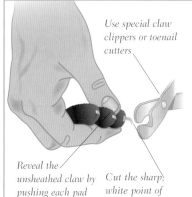

Use special claw clippers or toenail cutters

Reveal the unsheathed claw by pushing each pad

Cut the sharp, white point of each claw

Treatment Tips
Trimming claws

Trimming the claws must be done with care.

REVEAL THE UNSHEATHED CLAW
Holding the cat firmly, push the pad of each claw inward, one at a time. This will reveal the unsheathed claw.

FIND THE CUTTING LINE
The sharp, white point of the claw is the area to be trimmed. You need to cut the end of each claw using claw clippers, or ordinary toenail clippers.

However, once it has realized the purpose of the scratching post, the kitten should return here regularly to keep its claws in trim. In this way, your pet may scratch its claws in an acceptable way rather than on the side of a chair or other furniture.

How to train a kitten

Start by lifting your kitten's front legs up onto the post and pull them down, mimicking a scratching motion. You may also want to drape a toy down over the top of the post, to attract your cat's attention here—this should encourage it to start pawing at both the toy and the post behind.

Some toys encourage cats to pounce and exercise their claws while playing safely indoors.

Claws

Kittens' claws are especially sharp at their tips, because they have not been worn down like those of older cats. They also curl backward, so it is very important if you are lifting a kitten off a piece of fabric that you do not simply try to remove it straight from the material. Your kitten or cat will instinctively dig into the chairs with its claws, anchoring the material and probably damaging it by pulling a thread.

The safer option is to lift the cat a short distance off the chair and use your other hand to free the claws, before finally lifting the cat clear. It will be better to train your kitten or cat to sleep in a bed of its own if you are worried about damage to the furniture.

A rubber grooming pad for shorthaired cats.

It is always best to leave a cat's claws uncut, but regular trimming of the nails can help with a scratching problem indoors (a vet can show you how to do this using special claw clippers), or soft rubber or plastic covers obtained from the veterinarian can be placed over a cat's claws.

Hairs

Although regular grooming will help to remove many of the hairs being shed naturally from the coat, the number will increase during the molting period, in the spring, and then to a lesser extent in the early winter. Hairs build up on carpets and clothes. Some manufacturers now make special brushes to cope with the removal of pet hair.

Regular grooming is the best way to keep hairs away from furniture. A cat can also learn to sleep in its own bed rather than on other furniture.

dangers
in the kitchen

There are a surprising number of potential dangers lurking in the average kitchen, which could cause an injury or even death for a young kitten or new cat. It is a good idea to spend some time going around your home, looking for potential danger areas and taking steps to minimize the risk before acquiring your new pet.

Hazardous kitchens

In many homes, the kitchen is a busy thoroughfare, with family members coming and going through the door into the backyard, perhaps, or out to the garage. A kitten is often kept in a kitchen in its new home. This can help it to get used to the bustle of daily life but be aware that there are hazards. The kitten's things may take up space in the small kitchen causing congestion and accidents.

Take care with the positioning of the cat's bowls. Next to a cupboard that is frequently opened may not be the best place for a feeding area because a cat usually prefers to eat its meal without being disturbed.

The handle of a saucepan overhanging the surface could cause scalding

Hot plates may be a burning danger for a cat's paws

Items from the surface could fall off onto a cat

The open door of a washing machine may encourage a cat in

Also, a kitten may be in a draft when outside doors open and shut, so warmth and humidity may fluctuate dramatically in a kitchen area where the cooking is done.

The feeding area

If you are thinking of using the kitchen as a feeding area for your cat in the longer term, you need to consider the following:

• Household appliances such as washing machines and dryers can be upsetting for a cat at close quarters because of the noise they generate when operating.

• The position of food bowls close to worktops or drainers can cause accidents if items fall off surfaces.

• A cat demanding food while you are cooking can be hazardous—for instance, if you trip while you are carrying a pan full of boiling water.

• A cat may leap up on to the work surface to steal tidbits. This can be unhygienic if it is an area used to prepare human food.

• Some disinfectants used on work surfaces may be poisonous to cats, who absorb them or lick their feet.

• A cat may burn its paws by coming into contact with the hot burners of a stove.

• If a cat is a messy eater, the floor may need to be mopped frequently and may be slippery as a result.

The kitchen is a busy thoroughfare in many homes. Think carefully about the best place for cats to feed.

If you have a conservatory attached to the kitchen, it would be better to transfer your cat's food and water bowls here, along with its litter tray. Not only does this afford your pet more privacy, but it should also prove to be safer in the long run.

Safer kitchens

This may not be practical, however, so there are things that you can do to make the kitchen safer for you and your cat:
• Keep doors on refrigerators, washing machines, and tumble dryers closed so your cat cannot explore inside.

Always check your cat is not tucked up inside before using these sorts of appliances.
• Store items used for cooking (especially knives) and household goods safely away from cats in drawers or cupboards.
• Keep a firm lid on dangerous or toxic substances and store them away safely after use.
• Get rid of kitchen garbage safely (especially bottles, cans, bones, and scraps) preferably outside in a trash can that a cat cannot access.
• Close outer doors carefully—many cats get their tails caught in a door.

Dealing with scalds

If your cat is scalded in the kitchen or elsewhere:

1. Swab the wound with plenty of cold water or hold it under the faucet.

2. Make an ice pack and apply it to the scald.

3. Seek treatment for all but the most minor of scalds.

Do not apply butter or creams. Do not cover the wound or cut the fur. A little petroleum jelly can be used if your cat will allow it.

Cats like to find hiding places and a washing machine is an inviting place for a cat to sleep. Keep the door closed to avoid encouraging the cat to clamber inside just in case of accidents.

hazards
around the home

Kittens like to find new places to investigate.

All kittens and cats are explorers and because they are keenly territorial, they will want to investigate all parts of a house. If there are rooms that you would prefer your cat not to go in, you need to keep the door closed. If you have a balcony, you may need to keep your cat away from a possible fall. If there are dangers, you will need to be aware of them and act first. Sometimes accidents are caused when a cat demands affection or wants to investigate what its owner is doing, for example, jumping unexpectedly on a desk, knocking over a glass or an ornament with its paws or with the sweep of its tail.

Prevention is better than cure

These are some of the ways you can help prevent accidents around the home especially with a young cat that can climb and jump:

Living room

• Put all items that can be knocked off a shelf or table into a drawer, especially if they are breakable.

• Hide trailing cables, which may otherwise be gnawed with serious consequences. Unplug electrical appliances and place covers on unused electrical sockets when not in use.

• Secure a fireguard in front of the fireplace since a chimney is a tempting place for a nervous kitten.

• Keep plants out of reach unless they are safe for cats.

• Remove a dangling tablecloth.

Bedrooms

• Keep any medicines in a drawer or first-aid box (doses of aspirin, paracetamol, or laxatives, for example, can be very dangerous).

• Keep drawers and closets closed so that the cat cannot get shut in.

• Carefully store any small items that could be swallowed, such as hair clips, pins and needles, and elastic bands.

• Tidy away clothes and toiletries in drawers or closets.

Bathrooms

• Keep toilet and bathroom cleaners shut away in a cupboard because they may be poisonous.

• Keep the toilet lid closed to stop a cat from licking a dangerous cleaner.

• Never leave water in a sink or bathtub in case a kitten clambers in.

Garages

• Be aware of the dangers of motoring products such as antifreeze (see page 51) and other poisonous car liquids that may be stored there.

Left: Keep a cat away from the toilet bowl in case of dangerous cleaners inside.

Right: Always let the water out of a sink or bathtub before a cat climbs in.

Electric cables are attractive to kittens. Chewing through cables can cause burns to the mouth and paws and is often fatal.

Many town cats can become quite streetwise, but many are still killed on the roads, most commonly at night.

Many town cats can become quite streetwise, but many are still killed on the roads, most commonly at night.

those with sharp spines, such as cacti. Cats, especially those kept indoors, are liable to nibble vegetation. This may assist the digestive process, but cats can become quite ill if they eat any poisonous plants, such as dumb cane, which is highly fatal to both cats and small children. Cats that are allowed outside the house may nibble at grass so they may well leave the house plants alone.

If you have an indoor cat, cultivate a special container of grass that your cat can nibble at freely, so that it should hopefully leave other house-plants alone. Grass kits can be obtained from pet stores. They are usually made up of a container, seed, and soil, and the grass is easily grown on a windowsill. With regular watering, and plenty of light, the grass should last for several months.

• Keep decorating materials such as paint, cleaning spirits, and preservatives out of reach.
• Be aware that cats like to sleep under cars, especially with warm engines, either in a garage or in the road.

House plants

Care also needs to be taken with house plants including

The most common accident outside of the home is caused by traffic, and the injury is often serious.

House plants

Indoor plants that are toxic to cats include
• amaryllis
• ivies
• azalea
• caladium
• hydrangea
• umbrella plant
• rubber plant
• spider plant.
Indoor plants that are safe for cats include
• cyclamen • African violet • geranium • begonia.
Full lists can be obtained from your veterinarian's clinic.

festivities

with cats around

Your cat will share in your special occasions such as family gatherings, festivals, and celebrations. At these times, the household may be more chaotic than normal, and the usual routine is disrupted. Be aware of how these changes will affect your cat. Some cats will feel left out, or they may be frightened by the unexpected visitors and change in routine. Other cats like the extra tidbits, the treats, and the attention, and will often take advantage of the situation!

Common dangers

These are common dangers to be aware of at special occasions:

• Food: At Christmas, Thanksgiving, or other religious or seasonal festivals, there will probably be plenty of food in the home that appeals to cats—meat such as turkey, perhaps, or sausages. You need to be careful that your pet is not left unsupervised in the kitchen if food is left lying around.

Their delicate sense of smell can detect food on a work

There are plenty of treats on the market that you can give your pet if you wish.

surface from the kitchen floor. Cats may be poisoned by treats such as chocolate (theobromine), which does not agree with their digestive system.

Be careful with trash left over after a festive meal—cats may end up cutting their paws on sharp cans or choking on poultry bones. Bones can be especially dangerous, because they break easily into sharp fragments that can become stuck in a cat's throat.

• Tree and decorations: Many young cats find the colorful baubles on a Christmas tree especially irresistible, pawing at them until they are dislodged and fall off. If they are made of glass, they may break and injure your cat, so choose unbreakable plastic decorations for the lower part of the tree. Some cats will even try to climb a Christmas tree, so always ensure that it is mounted firmly in its container to prevent it from tipping over. In the upheaval caused by Christmas, avoid the temptation for a cat of using the earth base of a tree as a litter tray. If the tree is set in soil, cover it with logs or something similar, so that your cat cannot burrow into the earth. Also remember that many evergreens are poisonous to cats. A festive sprig of mistletoe is a poisonous plant for a cat.

• Lights: A young cat alone in a room will be attracted to an illuminated tree, particularly if the lights are flashing. A cat may be drawn not only to play with the lights but also to chew the electrical cable, so position the tree close to a power point and tuck the cable away as far as possible. Do not leave the tree unattended with the lights on. Also, be careful with lighted candles and special oils because your cat will not have a sense of danger concerning a naked flame until it is too late.

Some cats enjoy the extra food on offer at festive times. Keep aware of what your cat is being fed, and be careful that it does not take too much advantage of the situation.

• Fireworks: Fireworks are yet another hazard of the festive celebrations. Always be sure to call your pet inside before darkness falls if there are likely to be fireworks, because the noise and flashes of light terrify most cats. If left to its own devices, your cat will probably hide away from the noise and only emerge when it is all over.

• Barbecue: If you are holding a party with an outdoor barbecue, damp down the hot area once you have finished to prevent any risk of burns to cats on the prowl for food.

If your cat suffers a contact burn, either from a hot barbecue or even a hot burner in the kitchen, immediately run the blistered area under cold running water (also see page 105). Do not add ointment, lotions or butter to the blister. If the burn is serious, seek medical advice from your vet.

Be careful with chocolate.

allowing
your cat out

If you wish to let your cat out on a regular basis, you may decide to fit a pet door. This will allow your pet to come and go as it chooses. You can, of course, keep it confined indoors at night or whenever else you wish. There are a number of different types of pet door on the market. Some are very basic, while the more expensive designs offer security against other cats entering your home. In areas where cats are numerous, it is not unusual for another cat to enter your home through the pet door and steal your cat's food. Unfortunately unwelcome feline "visitors," especially tomcats, may also try to lay claim to your home as their territory by spraying.

Above: The decision as to whether to confine your cat to the house or allow it outside is often dictated by where you live. There are dangers in letting it out, but they have to weighed against the benefits of allowing your cat some freedom.

Left: Remember that while a pet door is a good way of providing your cat outdoor access it can also be an open invitation for other cats to come into your house if you are not careful.

You may mistakenly blame your own cat for soiling indoors, unaware of the unexpected visitors. Or if your cat is inside the home, you could suddenly be surprised by the sound of cats fighting in your kitchen.

Basic pet doors

Basic pet doors consist of a simple opening, in the form of a swinging flap, through which the cat enters and exits the home. You will need to check that the flap is conveniently sited, usually close to a back door (or within a panel of the door) and at a suitable height to allow your cat access through it.

With the more sophisticated designs, the cat wears a magnet on its collar so that access is denied to other cats. Before you invest in this type of door, check the cost and availability of replacement magnets because the cat will, no doubt, lose its collar at some point.

Learning to use the pet door

Detailed fitting instructions usually accompany pet doors, but generally these units are not difficult to fit in place. At first, however, you will need to show your cat how to use the flap, and you can develop this into a game. Try this:

1. Start by going outside, leaving your pet on the inside.
2. Call your cat, holding the flap slightly open so it can see the opening easily. You may need to lure a reluctant pet with a treat.

Since most pet doors open outward, coming back indoors can be more difficult for the cat. Depending on the design, the cat may need to use one of its front paws to lift the flap sufficiently for it to get its head underneath and go back inside.

Repeat the exercise with the pet door propped ajar, so that the cat can see through the opening. Its natural curiosity will probably be enough to persuade it to investigate under the flap and come back inside, especially if there is an offering of food there.

Above: Tempting your cat through the pet door with food provides good encouragement.

Left: You will need to show your cat how to use the pet door by holding it open.

Left: Most pet doors can be fitted according to the instructions. Most are lockable so you can shut your cat in at night. A lock can also keep unwanted cats from entering your house.

Treatment Tips
Pet-door deterrents

If you don't want other cats to use your pet door, here are some ways in which they may be deterred:

MAGNETIC PET DOORS
Can only be opened by a cat with a special magnetic activator.

LOCKING OR SEALING THE PET DOOR
Useful at night, when intruders may be most inclined to enter.

HUMANS AND DOGS
Both will deter a cat that may be frightened by indoor daytime activity.

dangers outside
for kittens

If you let your cat outside it is possible to have the best of two worlds. It can have a warm environment to return to indoors, but outside it can also stake out a territory, do a little hunting, exercise, and find a place to lie in the sun if it chooses. But the outside world is full of mysteries to a young cat, and there are a number of potential dangers here for the curious kitten and uninitiated hunter.

The first outdoor visit

Your kitten can go outside two weeks after it has had its final immunizations. Only allow your kitten out for short periods at first and accompany it around the yard. Keep a lookout for any other cats in the area. Your kitten will soon start to scent-mark its territory by rubbing its head against trees and fences. When you let it explore on its own, encourage it back into the house with food.

Dangers

When your kitten or cat is released into an exciting world of sights, sounds, and smells, be aware that there will be dangers from outdoor life. Some of these may be seasonal, but the sorts of dangers will be determined by what country and climate the cat lives in.

• Bees and wasps: These stinging insects are often a target for a kitten's hunting enthusiasm, and the young cat will not appreciate the risk of being stung until it is too late. A sting in the mouth can be very serious because the area here will swell up and may block off the windpipe. You will know if your pet has been stung because it will start pawing at its mouth and salivating excessively.

• Snake bites: Your cat could be at risk from snake bites, especially when they start to

Your kitten will be fascinated by what it finds in the backyard. Watch a kitten carefully so that it does not come to any danger or disappear out of sight. As it becomes more adventurous and curious, it may also become exposed to more dangers.

wander onto waste ground and seek out sunny spots to rest. In some parts of the world snakes bites are a common occurrence. In Europe, the adder is the only poisonous snake, recognized by the zig-zag markings running down its back. The major risk is often on a warm spring day in a temperate climate that has drawn a snake out of hibernation. It will seek out a sunny spot, but being less active, it may strike at your cat rather than getting away from it.

Remedy for stings and bites

• Stings: It is best to seek the advice of a veterinarian. In the case of a bee sting in or around the mouth, you may be able to reduce the effects by pulling out the sting as fast as possible. A magnifying glass should help to reveal the tiny dart that injected the poison, although the cat may have dislodged the sting itself by rubbing or biting at the area. As an emergency first-aid measure, bathe the site with a solution of sodium bicarbonate (baking soda), made with one level teaspoonful dissolved in a glass of warm water.

If your kitten is stung by a bee, it may be possible to remove the dart yourself. You should always tell your vet if your pet has been stung.

• Snake bites: It is usually possible to distinguish between a venomous and nonvenomous snake bite. The fangs of a nonvenomous snake leave a U-shaped bite impression, whereas venom causes much more severe swelling around two puncture wounds. If this happens, you need to get your cat to a veterinarian without delay so that it can be given antivenom.

First-aid for snake bites

Keep the cat as quiet as possible because if it becomes badly distressed the venom will be absorbed into the body at a faster rate. You can place a tourniquet at the top of the limb, using a clean piece of material. Allow about a finger's width directly under the tie, rather than knotting it tightly, and release the pressure after about 45 minutes to prevent the possibility of gangrene.

You can usually tell if a snake is poisonous by the bite it gives.

Case history

Jesse's young cat, Josie, had climbed a tree and was exploring among the branches. Unfortunately Josie disturbed a wasps' nest in the tree. Thinking this was a game she tried to chase the insects and catch them in her mouth as they flew off. Unfortunately in doing so one wasp stung her face. Josie, alarmed, frightened, and in pain, quickly jumped down from the branches and was found in a distressed state.

Jessie, realizing what had happened, took the correct action for the wasp sting, which, luckily, had not stung Josie in her mouth. Unlike a bee sting, which is acidic, wasp stings are alkaline, so Jesse bathed it in water and vinegar. Fortunately Josie did not have an allergic reaction to the sting itself, which would have needed immediate attention from the veterinarian. However, for peace of mind she also took Josie for a checkup.

ponds
and your kitten

Ponds may create dangers for kittens and cats because of the pond's likely occupants. Once they have become experienced hunters, cats often find it easy to catch amphibians such as frogs and toads.

Amphibians

Many frogs die as a result of being attacked by cats. But toads are better suited to life on land and defending themselves against would-be predators. An attack on a toad can make the cat quite ill. This is because toads have toxic skin secretions, released by the glands located towards the back of the head. When these secretions come into contact with the cat's mouth, they cause intense irritation. The cat drops the toad and

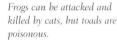

Frogs can be attacked and killed by cats, but toads are poisonous.

starts salivating profusely and foaming at the mouth. The cat usually recovers reasonably quickly, however, and soon learns to leave toads alone.

Gone fishing

The hunting instincts of cats, and especially young kittens, often extend to any fish in the pond. Brightly colored, tame fish that are kept in a garden pond come to surface readily for food and are tantalizing to a kitten. But kittens often find that it is much harder to scoop a fish out of a pond than to catch a butterfly on land, partly because the drag factor of the water slows the speed of its strike. This tilts the balance greatly in favor of the fish,

Tame fish such as carp in a pond may be tantalizing for a kitten.

Even a small pond of goldfish can be dangerous for a cat or kitten. A cat would find it quite difficult to get out of a pond like this if it fell in. It makes sense to cover ponds where possible, or keep cats away from them.

Water dangers

Most cats are not safe near
• swimming pools
• ponds
• lakes.
The only options are to cover the water with chicken wire or to fence them off. If this is not possible, it may be best to keep a cat in a cat run or indoors.

Kittens may chase butterflies in the garden and may even stand a good chance of trapping them.

It is safest to keep your kittens in at night by locking the pet door, especially if there are water dangers.

particularly if the pond is quite deep. But it will not stop a kitten or cat from trying, and it may end up falling into the water. Although cats can swim, it is not unknown for young kittens to drown, often because they become tired and cannot escape from the water. It is a good idea to have a slight ramp out of the pond—this helps not only your cat to reach dry land again easily but also other small, wild animals that could fall in. If your cat persists in trying to catch fish, try placing a mesh cover over the surface of the pond—after a while your pet will probably lose interest.

Problems with predators

Many owners worry about predators such as foxes attacking their cats, especially now that in some areas foxes are common in towns. A cat's natural agility means it can usually slip away from a fox quite easily. Cats can readily

climb to escape danger, darting along a fence in a way that a fox simply cannot match. Young kittens and disabled or older cats may be more vulnerable. If you are worried about your kitten or cat falling victim to a fox, or other wild predator such as coyote, bobcat, hawk, or owl, the best solution is to keep your cat indoors at night.

Many people think that wild animals such as foxes are a danger to cats but most cats are agile enough to escape easily.

constructing
a cat run

It is not difficult to build a cat run, and although it will be more time consuming than buying a ready-made unit, it will certainly be cheaper. It may even be possible to convert an existing outbuilding such as a shed. For owners and breeders of pedigree cats, making a self-built cat run may be an inconspicuous way of keeping cats safe. In places where there is legislation to protect wildlife against predation by cats, the building of such a shelter can be an important consideration.

Constructing the run

The run should be constructed from lumber approximately 2in. (50mm) square, and it is important that it is weather-proofed to extend the lifespan of the structure. It will save time to buy "tanalized" timber, which means it is pretreated

under pressure—the preservative is forced into the wood more effectively than if it were applied with a brush. If you have to cut the lumber the joints will need to be treated separately and must be allowed to dry thoroughly before you allow the cat or cats into the enclosure.

To build the run

• Assembling the framework and panel: Use screws to assemble the framework, then lay each panel flat on a firm surface so you can attach the mesh. This should be approximately 1in. (2.54cm) square, with a strand thickness of 16 gage.

• Attaching the mesh: The mesh needs to be cut carefully so there are no loose ends that could injure your cat.

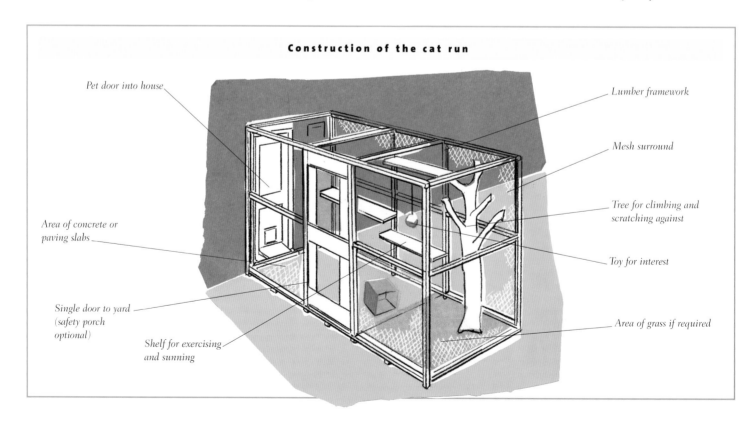

Construction of the cat run

Pet door into house

Lumber framework

Mesh surround

Tree for climbing and scratching against

Area of concrete or paving slabs

Toy for interest

Single door to yard (safety porch optional)

Shelf for exercising and sunning

Area of grass if required

Either cut the vertical strands back tightly against the horizontal strand above, or simply fold the cut ends around the adjoining lumber face, where they can be knocked flat and will be out of reach once the frames are assembled. Choose special netting staples for attaching the mesh, and drive them into the wood at intervals of approximately 2in. (5cm).

• Building the trench and wall: Trenches for the foundations of the run need to be dug at least 18in. (45cm) below ground level. A blockwork or brick wall should be extended up for a similar distance above the ground, right around the perimeter of the run, to support the framework. The frames are easily attached to this base with frame-fixers, but prepare the base for the run first.

A self-built cat run may be a way of allowing your cat some independence while you are out at work. It is also an inconspicuous way of keeping cats safe.

• Preparing the base: Be aware that a grass base will soon become muddy, and it will be difficult to keep it clean. Concrete or paving slabs are better options, since these can be hosed down and disinfected as required. Bear in mind that concrete is obviously a more permanent option than paving slabs. The floor covering needs to slope away from the shelter for drainage purposes.

Case history

Doreen was the owner of four pedigree kittens. She was keeping the kittens indoors, but was looking for space to expand and also allow the cats more freedom as they grew. She wanted to give them the option of being able to go outside when they wanted to, but because they were valuable, they also needed to be kept safe from theft. Her answer was to construct a purpose-built cat run in the yard, annexed off the house so that it looked rather like a small conservatory. This inconspicuous building would allow her cats access through a window to the cat run, so that they could come in to the house in poor weather and would also be safe at night. Although the yard was secluded, a firm lock on the outside of the cat run would also help to keep the run safe.

• Doors: The arrangement of the doors in the structure is important if you intend to incorporate a safety porch to stop the cat from running out. The outer door, leading into the porch, should open outward to give ease of access, while the inner door should open into the run itself, with a secure bolt on the inner face of the door. Externally, there should be a padlock to keep the door firmly locked, so that potential thieves are discouraged from entering the run.

Finish the run by adding items of interest for a cat, such as elevated shelves to sit on. You can also add solidly built toys or those that can dangle from the roof. A tree trunk to climb on or to scratch would be an ideal addition to a run.

A cat will be safe in a cat run.

protection
from the weather

Some breeds of cats are better suited to the cold than others. Norwegian Forest cats are well adapted to living in a relatively harsh climate. This is because they have evolved in their natural environment over the course of centuries, rather than having been selectively bred for their looks. Their thick, weather-resistant coat means they can survive outdoors even when the weather is very cold, thanks in part to the dense underfur that holds body heat close to the skin.

Other cats, such as the Siamese, which evolved naturally in tropical parts of the world, have a very different coat structure. They do not have a dense undercoat, while their top coat is sleek and lies flat, emphasizing the natural contours of the cat's body. More extreme examples are the Rex breeds, and particularly the Sphynx. These are cats that have evolved from natural mutations and have very sparse coats that give them little protection against the elements.

The Norwegian Forest cat has evolved a long, thick coat which was designed to be its protection during a long Scandinavian winter.

Most shorthairs will venture out in cold weather. Their fur thickens during the winter months and they start to molt as the weather gets warmer.

Outdoor protection

In temperate climates, it is important to protect the cat from the winter cold in an outdoor run. This can be done partly by roofing over the first section of the run closest to the shelter, extending down the sides as well, with a cat flap giving easy access to and from the attached shelter. The shelter needs to be welllit and ventilated.

An infrared heat lamp suspended from the roof will provide a warm spot for your cat, or you may prefer to install the type of convector heater often used in greenhouses. This can be thermostatically controlled to minimize heating costs. As with all electrical equipment, it needs to be adequately protected, so the cat cannot burn itself or spray urine over the heater. A snug bed raised on a shelf just off the floor of this sheltered area will help to keep your pet out of a draft.

Siamese cats evolved in tropical parts of the world so they have only thin coats that do not provide them with much protection from the weather.

A Siamese is more suited to summer.

Cats in the cold

If your cat is roaming freely outdoors in cold weather, do not allow it to stay out for longer than it needs to, particularly if it has a fine coat. Also, bear in mind that a cat can be vulnerable outdoors, especially if it is close to water. If your cat decides to chase a bird across a thin layer of ice on a pond, it could end up falling through the ice and, weighted down by wet fur, be unable to scramble to safety.

Hot spots

In hot climates or in the summer season in temperate climates, cats are also vulnerable to heat. Those with white fur are particularly at risk. Their underlying skin is pink and has little defense against the sun's radiation, leaving them highly susceptible to sunburn. Even black-coated cats are at risk if their ears are white, and sunburn can lead to skin cancer. Try to keep your pet indoors when the sun is at its hottest, because cats like to sunbathe.

Treatment Tips
Sunburn and heat stroke

SUNBURN
Occurs on ear tips and noses of white cats. Keep cats indoors and out of the sun if possible. Sunscreens made especially for cats are available but will need reapplying regularly.

HEAT STROKE
Heat exhaustion can occur in cats, especially those left in hot cars. The cat will pant heavily and will eventually collapse. Give the cat a cool bath and immediately seek the advice of a veterinarian.

boarding
your cat

If you decide to take a vacation, you need to have made arrangements about boarding your cat. Your cat may stay at special pet hotels, centers, or boarding catteries.

Wherever you choose to board your cat, it is always useful to follow recommendations from friends or neighbors. You can obtain lists of local facilities or search the Internet. Where possible, arrange a visit to the establishment first so that you can see the what is on offer before making a firm booking. Things to look for include:

• Clean premises, with well-trained and caring staff.

• Own quarters: You should also ensure that your cat will have its own quarters although cats from the same family will probably be housed together.

• Requests for immunization certificates. This is a sign that it has good standards of health care.

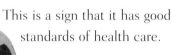

Above: Arrange to visit some catteries before you decide which one to put your cat in. Good catteries get booked up early for the vacation season.

Above: Take along your cat's favorite toy to play with at the boarding establishment.

Right: Your cat will get used to a boarding establishment after initially finding the experience quite stressful. It is not uncommon for a cat to lose interest in its food for a day or two, before it settles down.

Even in the best-run establishments, cats often find living in new surroundings quite stressful initially. It is very important to let the owners know the type of food your cat prefers, or whether it requires any sort of medication or special prescription diet. You should check that your cat is free from fleas or parasites and treat it before you take your cat to be boarded. Skin, coat, ears, and eyes should all be in a healthy condition. You should expect the boarding establishment to give the cat a health check before allowing it to stay. If possible, take along a favorite toy or blanket that your cat associates with home and a favorite treat.

Friends and neighbors

With older cats, or those that are suffering from a chronic illness, not only may a boarding establishment be reluctant to take them, but their conditions may also deteriorate. It might be possible to persuade a friend or neighbor to come in and see to the needs of your pet while you are away.

If you leave your cat behind, it must be adept at using its pet door to come in and out on its own. Should your cat become lonely, there is a risk that it may wander off if you are gone for more than a day or so.

Pet sitters

You may want to employ a pet sitter to look after your cat and any other pets you may have, as well as your home, while you are away. You should always check them out carefully and inform your insurance company. Most pet-sitter services operate on a daily rate, depending on the number of cats and other pets in the household.

Unless you are very unlucky, your pet should be in safe hands while you are away.

Advertisements for pet sitters can be found in magazines.

Unfortunately, it is rarely practical to take a cat with you on vacation. Most cats become upset by the journey and will not react well to being in strange surroundings. There is a chance that they may run away and disappear in a strange area.

What to pack

Take advice from the boarding establishment, but usually your cat will need
- a secure cat carrier
- separate bedding
- a favorite toy
- vaccination certificates
- contact information
- details of diet and/or medication for your cat.

your cat
and her kittens

A female cat will be able to have kittens from an early age if she is not neutered. If you wish to have your female cat spayed, it is best if it is carried out before she is five months old, when she will start calling. (Neutering is also an important consideration for males and should be carried out before they are about six months old.)

Planned pregnancy

You should not just allow your cat to become pregnant without organizing a suitable stud cat to sire the kittens and finding good homes for the offspring. Every year, many kittens are doomed to premature deaths because of thoughtless breeding. An unneutered young female cat is almost certain to become pregnant very quickly, especially is she is allowed to roam in an urban area.

1. Signs of pregnancy

A number of males may pursue a single female, and it is quite possible for her to give birth to kittens in the same litter sired by different fathers. This is why, if you take your queen to stud, she must not be allowed out immediately on your return because she may mate again unexpectedly.

The fact that ovulation has occurred can usually be seen from a change in the queen's behaviour—she stops calling. If mating does not occur, she will continue to call for ten days or more. Should pregnancy not have occurred, then after a further week or so she will come back into pro-estrus; otherwise, there will be no signs of sexual behavior until after the kittens are born.

2. The physical changes

Within the queen's body, the fertilized ova travel down to the uterus, where they implant in the wall, ultimately forming a placental connection that will nourish the

Left: The mother is a source of food, warmth, and comfort to her young kittens.

Below: If the mother wishes to move her kittens she carries each one gently in her mouth.

developing kittens through until birth. Never be tempted to press hard on the walls of the queen's abdomen to see if you can detect the developing fetuses, however, because this could kill them and injure the queen herself. It is not possible to detect the number of kittens reliably in this way in any case. About three weeks into the pregnancy, you will notice that the queen's nipples are becoming more prominent.

Birthing

When a queen gives birth you will need to have ready
- kittening box
- bedding
- hot-water bottle
- bowl of warm water
- gauze and cotton wool
- feeding bottle
- antiseptic
- milk feed
- cotton
- scissors.

Above: The kittens find their way to the queen's nipples to feed.

Right: Make sure the queen eats well, and uses her litter tray.

3. Preparing for the birth

Make preparations for the birth at an early stage, so the queen will feel comfortable with them. Try to persuade her to use a kittening box, placed in a quiet part of the house. This can be as basic as a cardboard box lined with old material, and placed on its side. She may well have other ideas, however, so watch her closely and respond to her needs, placing the kittening box where she seems to be spending long periods of time. Otherwise, you may find that she gives birth in a drawer, or even under a bed. Be wary about letting her out toward the end of pregnancy, too, since she may wander off and give birth elsewhere, such as in a shed.

4. The birth

The kittens are normally born head first, but if you are worried at any stage during the process, contact your vet for advice. Try not to disturb the queen unless absolutely necessary, because this is likely to result in her moving the kittens soon after birth, carrying them by the scruff of the neck to a location where she feels more secure.

Above: A queen usually gives birth to up to six kittens, which grow up together as part of a litter.

raising *kittens*

Once the kittens are born, it is important that they start feeding as soon as possible, so that they can gain the most benefit from their mother's colostrum. This milk contains protective antibodies, that can be absorbed directly across the intestinal wall and into a kitten's body. This gives vital protection during the first 48 hours that will last until the kitten's own immune system is fully functional at about three months of age. If for any reason a kitten fails to receive any colostrum, it is likely to be far more susceptible to illness than would otherwise be the case, often failing to thrive.

The kittens should start to feed from the queen as soon as possible after the litter is born.

Feeding

The kittens move instinctively towards their mother's nipples soon after birth. Although they are blind and virtually helpless, they can manage to wriggle along, paddling their legs, before nestling in the fur to find a nipple. The queen may not allow a newborn kitten to start feeding, however, until the whole litter has been born. This is more likely if she has not given birth before, since she will probably be more nervous. Usually, however, queens make excellent mothers and need little help from onlookers.

By the time the kittens are just a couple of days old, a teat dominance has formed. The rear teats produce more

milk; so the kittens that suckle here will develop faster and are likely to end up slightly larger than the others in the litter. The queen will lick her offspring frequently while they are still blind and helpless, especially after they have fed, to encourage them to relieve themselves.

Early care

A queen may move her litter around the home. This mimics the way in which wildcats act, to make it harder for predators to find the litter by observing the female when she returns to her offspring. This may keep on happening until the kittens are five weeks old.

This kitten is just beginning to explore the world around it.

Young kittens like to curl up together to sleep.

The queen, however, should not stray far. Beware if you are having any building works done in the house, however, because she will be tempted to hide her litter under the floorboards if an opportunity presents itself, and it is likely to prove very difficult to retrieve them.

The needs of the queen

The queen must be provided with plenty of drinking water. While she is suckling her litter she will drink far more than usual. It is also important to feed her more often, so that her body will not lose body condition while raising her kittens. She will need about twice her usual ration of food, split into three or four meals daily. Make sure that her milk is flowing smoothly when she feeds the kittens.

Treatment Tips
Early development

THE FIRST FEW DAYS

When the kittens are born they are blind and deaf. They are nursed within the first few hours and may feed for eight hours a day. The kittens use touch and warmth to find food. By four days they have some ability to move.

ONE TO TWO WEEKS OLD

The kittens' eyes open (each eye may open separately).

Kittens initiate feeding by kneading their paws and purring. The mother stimulates their toilet habits by licking. The kittens begin to move toward sounds.

TWO TO THREE WEEKS OLD

The kittens' outer ears straighten. By the third week, the kittens begin to crawl. Their sense of smell improves and they can now see their mother.

weaning
behavior

Once the kittens are about three weeks of age, they will be moving around and will start to sample food from their mother's dish. At this stage, you can begin to offer the kittens small amounts of milky food, such as special cat's milk, sold in pet stores. From about a month onward, they can be introduced to more solid food—special kitten food is readily available. Even at this early stage, there is likely to be a noticeable difference between breeds—shorthaired breeds, such as the Siamese, are more advanced in terms of development than the slow-maturing longhairs, such as Persians.

Starting on solids

The female cat will start to lose interest in suckling her offspring when they start to take more solid food. This in turn causes her milk flow to start drying up, so there is less available to the kittens. There is a risk at this stage that the queen may wander off and mate again, so keep a close watch on her.

As the kittens start to take solid food, ensure that they do not develop diarrhea. This is serious in young cats because they will dehydrate rapidly, and any infection can spread easily through the entire litter. It can be helpful to use a probiotic at this stage, to minimize the risk of any

A kitten should not be given an adult cat's meal at first. Commercial weaning diets are available and kittens should be fed a little food often as their stomachs are small.

By about eight weeks, kittens should be encouraged to give up their mother's milk. They should always have plenty of water available.

digestive upset. Probiotics contain beneficial bacteria, which maintain the population within the digestive tract, making it harder for any pathogenic organisms to become established and cause disease. Probiotics in powdered form can be bought from many pet stores, and they are simply given by sprinkling over the food in accordance with the instructions on the package.

When feeding the kittens, it is important to supervise them, to ensure that they all receive a share. It may also be a good idea to feed them when their mother is elsewhere, because she may decide that she prefers their food to hers, and eat it all herself.

Sexing and worming

A litter of purebred kittens is registered at birth. At this stage, sexing needs to be carried out carefully, so if you are in doubt, check with your veterinarian. Do not automatically assume that a tortoiseshell kitten in a litter is female.

These kittens have developed all their senses. By the time they are six weeks old they should be able to eat regular food. It can be easier to feed kittens when the mother is not around, so all the kittens get their fair share of the food.

Treatment Tips

Development at weaning

FOUR TO FIVE WEEKS OLD

Kittens begin to learn to use the litter tray. Hearing and reflexes become much stronger. Active play occurs with litter-mates. Much improved vision. Self-grooming starts. Body temperature is controlled through licking. Mothers start to bring live prey.

SIX TO SEVEN WEEKS OLD

Kittens develop a keen sense of smell and sight. Baby teeth grow. Mutual grooming takes place in litter. Feeding on solid food begins. Kittens may start to kill mice (see pages 128–129).

They usually are, for genetic reasons, but males are not unknown and do crop up occasionally, although they are infertile.

Young kittens can be vulnerable to roundworms, so seek advice from your veterinarian on deworming. Deworming will start when they are about a month old, and then continues at monthly intervals up to the age of six months old. After this, cats that roam freely and hunt should be treated every six months. Since the queen can transmit roundworms to her offspring, she too should ideally have been wormed just before mating.

the socialization
of the litter

The bonds formed between kittens will last throughout their lives if they stay together as a colony. Their mother, too, will remain close to her kittens if the group is not separated, with the cats often spending time together resting during the day, as well as grooming each other. Mutual grooming in cats is not common and reflects a close relationship between the mother and her litter. If they are still a family group when they are sexually mature, the toms wander off for intervals during the breeding season, but although they may disappear for days or even weeks, they will still be accepted back into the group when they return.

In the wild

It is usual in the case of wildcats for family groups to remain together for months, if not years, after weaning. The young can learn and practise the skills they need to survive in the wild. Their mother begins to train them as they approach independence, bringing back injured prey for her offspring to catch and kill. This is the natural way in which young cats start to refine their natural instincts. They start to go with the mother on hunting expeditions.

Above: In the wild, big cats stay together with their mothers for longer than smaller cat species. This is because they need strength and ability to attack large and dangerous prey, and may not be able to achieve this by themselves until they are full-grown.

Left: If kittens stay together, the bond between them remains. Mutual grooming is an indication that there is a close relationship between the cats.

The kittens learn from their mother by following her example. Although at first the young cats are likely to reduce their mother's hunting success, they soon learn to hide themselves. She will watch over them, alerting them

to danger by a low-pitched growl, to which they respond immediately by staying very still, in the hope of avoiding conflict with a larger predator. If they become separated from their mother, the young cats can utter calls in the ultra-sound part of the range, which although inaudible to human ears can be detected by their mother, who can retrace her steps to find her offspring.

As far as wildcats are concerned, the young of large species such as tigers spend longer in the company of their mothers than those of smaller members of the family. This is a reflection of the fact that large cats must tackle bigger and more dangerous prey, which could cripple or even kill a young tiger outright if it does not possess the strength to overpower it. Furthermore, until the young cat has shed its

All young cats have an instinct to hunt.

milk teeth and grown permanent canine teeth, it will not be able to kill its prey effectively.

Hunting games

Kittens will enjoy games such as these because they mimic the hunting instinct
• Roll a ball or other item for your kitten to chase.

• Provide a catnip toy for your kitten to toss.

• Play a fishing-rod game so your kitten can pounce.

Socialization with humans

Because they are raised with a breeder at home or in a cattery, many domestic cats do not have the wildcat's opportunity to refine their hunting skills. When raising kittens at home, the socialization period is important for bonding with people as well as the rest of the litter.

This bonding period starts about the time a kitten opens its eyes at under two weeks old and continues until it is about seven weeks old. A kitten's vision, sense of smell, hearing, and reflexes all develop during this sensitive stage, and early stimulation has been proved to help brain cells to grow. Social bonds are formed within the litter through mutual grooming and this activity holds them together for as long as they are kept together. It is thought that the more kittens are talked to, stroked, and handled at this early stage, the easier it is for them to bond with humans. The comfort that comes from a mother licking her kittens, and from kittens licking each other, finally comes from being stroked by us. After the socialization period has ended, the mother and her litter are usually separated.

keeping a
cat healthy

A domesticated cat has few of the health hazards that are faced by its wild or feral relatives. You can make sure that your pet has a clean and safe environment in which to live by following some simple procedures. Vacuuming, cleaning, and safe disinfecting of your home all help to keep the living area free of germs and your pet healthy. Routine checkups, vaccinations and neutering may be the only visits to the veterinarian that are required for a healthy cat.

Health check

These are some simple things you can do to check your cat is healthy. Check the following on a regular basis:

• Coat: It should feel dry and smell clean, with no sign of fleas, lice, or ticks (see pages 132–133).

• Ears: They should smell and look clean, with no dark specks or gray-brown wax caused by the presence of ear mites (also see pages 132–133).

Above: A healthy cat will have clear eyes with no discharge from the eyes, ears, or nose. Regular checks will help to make sure that any symptoms of sickness are noticed.

Right: Take your cat to the vet for expert advice if you are at all worried about its health.

Most cats stay very healthy, but they will need yearly inoculations and health checks.

• Skin: There should be no bald or scaly patches or pustules on the skin indicating ringworm, dermatitis, or eczema.

• Teeth: They should look clean and white and none should be loose. The breath should smell sweet indicating there is no problems with the gums (see pages 94–95).

• Eyes: They should be bright and clear, with no haws (third eyelids) visible except when blinking.

• Mouth: The gums and tongue should be pink, and there should be no inflammation of the gums or abscesses (see pages 94–95).

Symptoms

Signs of illness include
• sneezing
• coughing
• a wet or runny nose
• tearful eyes
• a scruffy coat
• persistent vomiting
• diarrhea
• unaccustomed spraying
• labored breathing
• lameness
• loss of balance
• bad-temperedness
• listlessness.

Inspecting the ears for ear mites.

A bald patch may just be caused by rubbing or could be parasites.

• Under the tail: The anal area should be clean. If it is not clean, diarrhea may be the cause.
• Body: There should be no odd lumps and bumps around the body.
• Paws: There should be no soreness or cracking.

Signs of sickness

All living creatures are prone to accidents or illness. Becoming familiar with your own pet and carrying out regular health checks can help you to know when something is not quite right. Some of the changes in behavior that occur when a cat is ill can be quite subtle, such as excessive thirst.

Generally, a first sign that all is not well is a lack of interest in food (also see pages 84–85). However, stress or a change in routine can also have the same effect. If there appears to be a problem, the cat should be kept indoors and under close observation. No medicines should be given without the advice of the veterinarian.

To the clinic

Some signs of illness are so obvious that you know you have to take the cat to the clinic immediately. Before getting in the car, it is best to phone the veterinarian, describe the symptoms, and let the clinic know that you are coming. You should take the cat to the clinic in its carrier, and not open it until you are in the consulting rooms. The veterinarian will diagnose the problem and provide the necessary treatment. It is worth remembering that nursing a sick cat at home is not easy, and if a cat is seriously unwell it is best if it is cared for at the clinic.

Take your cat to the veterinarian in a secure carrier if you suspect it might be unwell.

parasites
and your cat

Cats that are allowed outside are most at risk from parasites. Fleas are the most common type of parasite that affects cats. Such is their reproductive rate that it takes just a single female flea to cause an epidemic. Fleas need a warm environment to breed but will only do so outdoors in semi-tropical countries. Although flea numbers tend to peak in the summer in temperate countries, they can be a year-round problem in centrally heated homes.

The life cycle of a flea

The flea will lay her eggs on the cat's coat, and these will fall off, often in the areas where the cat sleeps regularly. The eggs hatch into larvae, which live on the floor, hidden in the carpeting, before entering the inert pupal stage of their life cycle. Finally, they hatch into adult fleas, leaping up onto anything that passes, be it a cat or your leg. Since fleas are largely inconspicuous until their numbers have increased dramatically, it is always important to be aware of the possibility of fleas on your pet. Very young cats can also have fleas. They can move between dogs and cats, so if you have both you will need to treat both (check the

Ticks are wingless, blood-sucking insects. They attach themselves to the skin of an animal and fill their bodies with blood in one large meal. Ticks are most commonly found on cats that live in the country, where they pick them up from other animals, or from long grasses.

instructions for use carefully on flea-killing products, since those intended for dogs can be harmful to cats, and especially kittens in some cases).

Life cycle of the flea

Eggs are laid by the adult female flea living on a cat

The pupae wait in their cocoons for cat to pass. They hatch out in seconds and jump on to a passing cat

The eggs drop on to the carpet on the floor where they hatch

Larvae hide in the home and form pupae

Treatment

If you detect fleas on your cat (see pages 84–85), it will not just be a matter of treating your cat, but also cleaning its environment thoroughly to minimize the risk of reinfection. Fleas can also be the host for an infestation of tapeworm (fleas eat tapeworm eggs, the cat eats the fleas and the eggs are released into the cat's intestines where tapeworms share its food). To remove fleas, start by washing the bedding, and vacuuming to remove the immature

Fleas are to be suspected if your cat is scratching a lot on the back of its head and the base of the spine.

• Ticks: These are picked up from long grasses. The tick buries itself in a cat's skin and remains there until it fills with blood. The tick can be removed with an insecticidal spray, or carefully with tweezers (including the embedded head) if the area is anesthetized with alcohol first.

The earlier the signs of infestation are spotted the better. Take your cat to the clinic as soon as possible if you suspect an infestation and are not happy removing ticks yourself. Ticks can also carry disease to humans.

stages in the life cycle from the carpeting before using the flea treatments available. It is important to act fast, because where fleas build up in the home to epidemic proportions, the only way to control them will be to call in a specialist pest-control team. Other types of parasite that can infect your cat are:

• Ear mites: If the cat keeps scratching its ear or shaking its head it may have ear mites, which can cause irritation and inflammation in the ear canal. The ear can be cleaned and treated by the vet, who will also prescribe ear drops.

Treatment Tips
Flea treatments

INSECTICIDES
Powders, "spot-on" preparations, and aerosol sprays can be used to kill the infestation. Products from your veterinarian will be the best.

ORAL TREATMENTS
These are given to your cat as a small liquid dose. The active ingredient is slowly absorbed into the cat's bloodstream.

Any flea that bites your cat will produce eggs that are nonviable. Treatments should be available from your veterinarian.

FLEA COLLARS
Flea collars (with insecticide) can be bought, but are not very effective. They may also cause irritation or an allergy around the cat's neck.

better behavior

4 Cats are all individuals, and they react in different ways to the world around them. Sometimes bad habits begun during kittenhood can become established as part of a cat's behavior. This may cause more problems in later life. For instance, while it may be fun having a kitten that tries to pounce on your hand as you move your fingers along in front of its face, this can be a very painful experience with an adult cat. Most behavioral problems develop slowly, and the circumstances that led to the cat developing the behavior may not be easily remembered later. The situation is likely to be most difficult in the case of an adult cat, particularly a stray, since the problem may not actually surface until the cat is living in a new owner's home. This section looks at how some behavioral problems in cats can be identified and remedied.

the owner's
responsibilities

When you start out with a kitten, try to have some consistent guidelines from the outset. If, for example, you do not want your cat to sit on a sofa, then do not encourage this behavior while it is a cute kitten and then expect it to desist once it is older. Breaking the habit at this stage will be very difficult, whereas if the cat has never been actively encouraged to sleep on a chair, but always in its own bed, then this problem will not develop.

Cats need consistent rules. Unless you have made it clear that a cat should not jump up at mealtimes, a cat will not hesitate to jump up to your plate if it is unattended.

Reinforcing the rules

Always teach your kitten to play gently, establishing guidelines again, and scold it immediately if it starts to bite or scratch. If this happens within the confines of a game, then stop playing with your pet immediately and ignore it. Cats soon come to realize that this behavior is not acceptable, especially if you break off the game without any delay at this stage.

There is no point in reacting some time after an event. Your pet will not be able to understand why it is being punished, and it will just serve to weaken the bond between you. Cats are very sensitive creatures, and your tone of voice can be very effective when it comes to expressing your displeasure. If the cat climbs on to the dinner table, you must respond at once so that the cat can associate the cause with the effect of its action.

Above: Encourage your cat to play with its own toys rather than household objects or personal possessions.

Right: You need to make a clear and immediate distinction between what you allow your cat to play with and what is out of bounds.

Treatment Tips
Training cats

INTIMIDATION

This involves making a loud noise when unwanted behavior is directed toward you. If your cat uses your leg as a scratching post, raising your voice will deter the behavior from happening on another occasion.

INDIRECT PUNISHMENT

This is when your cat is deterred from an activity without associating you with the training. For example, if you wish to stop the cat from scratching the furniture, a surprise jet of water from a water pistol (without being seen yourself) is a method known to produce good results.

Overcoming problems

If you find that you have what appears to be a persistent problem with your cat, it is important to seek advice without delay. The longer a problem is allowed to develop unchecked, the harder it will be to overcome it. There is little point in blaming your cat simply because some of the fault is likely to be on your part. The good news, however, is that in many cases, although it will take time and patience, it is usually possible to correct your cat's behavior. Some behavioral problems, such as wool-sucking (see pages 140–141), are more commonly associated with some breeds than others. Sometimes difficulties are not generally regarded as inherited problems, but are thought to be linked to the cat's early experiences in life. Always bear in mind that changes in your working pattern, or a move, are likely to impact on your cat's behavior as well.

Finally, always be sure to spend time with your cat, because otherwise the cat may start to become bored, and this can also lead to vices developing. Always allow sufficient time to play with your cat every day.

Top to bottom right: Indirect punishment is carried out when you wish to persuade a cat from carrying out an undesirable action such as climbing on or scratching the furniture. A surprise shot of water (1), (2) and (3) makes the cat move off the furniture and deters it from climbing on to it again in the future.

finding the cause of a
cat's stress

Just like ourselves, cats can suffer from stress. This is actually a measurable physiological condition, rather than simply a mental condition, and reflects the way in which a cat reacts to significant changes in its environment. Some cats are more vulnerable to stress than others, depending on their temperament. If your cat is instinctively nervous, then the likelihood is that it will be more vulnerable to stress. The problem may be manifested in a number of ways, with the cat hiding away, or sometimes becoming aggressive if it feels trapped, losing its appetite, or even soiling in the house.

Identifying the cause

If your cat starts to behave strangely, it is important to try to pinpoint when the behavior first occurred, and what might have triggered it.

These are common causes of stress:

• Cat carrier: In the case of many normally placid cats, the sight of a cat carrier can be distressing. This is because in the cat's mind it is linked with unpleasant journeys to the veterinarian's clinic, with the cat often feeling stressed simply as a result of the journey itself. Once it realizes what is happening, your cat is likely to try to run out of the house or hide from you.

Try using the carrier in the home without it being associated with a journey. It may help to associate the carrier with something pleasant such as food. Try to get your cat used to its carrier while it is still a kitten.

A visit to the vet is a stressful experience for most cats. Your vet will realize that your pet is likely to be upset and will handle the cat as gently as possible.

If a cat is frightened, perhaps because it has been scared by thunder, or is feeling unwell, then it will often hide away.

• Traveling: Accustoming your kitten to short car journeys at an early stage will help to overcome its fear of traveling. It will simply be a matter of taking the kitten out in its carrier and driving around for five minutes or so, before returning home. Try to schedule this just before the kitten's mealtime—it will be less likely to suffer from travel sickness, and will be distracted from its experience by food offered immediately on its return.

Although there is a widespread belief that cats always dislike traveling in cars, experienced show cats frequently travel long distances by road without becoming upset, having become used to car travel from an early age.

Helping stress

Try to alleviate the causes
of stress by
• exercise
• play
• stroking
• herbal remedies
• Bach Flower Remedies
• diet
• medication.
It helps also to keep to a
cat's normal routine.

Visiting the veterinarian

Kittens are especially impressionable to bad experiences. If it has just endured a journey to the clinic, you need to be careful it is not confronted by other people's inquisitive or aggressive pets in the waiting room. It is always better to leave the kitten in its carrier to calm down after the journey, without subjecting it to another trauma and taking it out of its carrier. Otherwise a kitten may become so distressed that it will attack its owner and become quite uncontrollable, looking for any way out of the room and disappearing from sight. A kitten that behaves in this way will be very hard to find until it calms down and becomes hungry, since it is most likely to hide away once it reaches what it considers to be a safe haven.

*Always take your
cat to the clinic in
a secure carrier, and
keep it away
from dogs.*

problems
with grooming

All cats should be accustomed to being groomed from an early age, and this is especially important in the case of longhaired breeds. If this vital aspect of their care is neglected, the coat can become matted. Grooming is then likely to prove painful for the cat, with the comb or brush pulling at the hair. In extreme cases, it may be necessary to sedate a cat with a badly matted coat so that the mats can be cut out. Attempting to remove them by grooming will be

It is healthy for all cats, including shorthairs, to become accustomed to grooming from an early age.

Right: A shorthaired cat will benefit from being brushed at least once a week. Once the matted parts have been removed with a comb, a brush can have a soothing effect on a cat's skin.

Below: Since most cats enjoy being stroked, good brushing can be a pleasurable experience.

too upsetting for the cat, and can lead to persistent grooming problems in the future.

You are not likely to have a grooming problem with a cat that has grown up with you since kittenhood. Grooming difficulties can occur in older cats that have been rehomed because they may have been neglected in the past.

Treatment Tips
The key to grooming

BEGIN YOUNG
Your cat should enjoy its grooming sessions.

GROOM REGULARLY
This will avoid knots and a matted coat, which makes grooming painful for the cat and difficult to handle.

A PROBLEM COAT
Improve a very badly matted coat when the cat is under sedation. Begin the process of proper grooming again.

These cats will need to be handled carefully when being groomed, because they may strike at you, not because they are in pain but simply out of fear. Such cats will invariably struggle fiercely to try to escape when being held for grooming, even if they do not attempt to bite and scratch.

If you are adopting a cat from a shelter, and are worried about this, ask the staff to let you see how easy it will be to groom the cat before deciding whether or not you will be able to manage it. With patience, it should be possible in time to overcome your cat's fear to a great extent. At first you are likely to need someone else to hold the cat for you while you concentrate on grooming. If it starts to play up, try holding the cat firmly by the scruff of the neck, allowing you to continue the process.

In due course, as the cat is groomed every day, it will come to realize that it is not a painful procedure and its fear will lessen, although you need to take care if the coat does start to become tangled.

Wool-sucking

Some cats can become obsessive about grooming themselves, to the extent that they lick areas of the coat so much that they start to become inflamed.

This is often linked with what is described as wool-sucking, when a cat sucks at a piece of bedding. This may be comfort sucking, related to an earlier weaning problem. It is quite common in Siamese cats from about six months of age, and although some cats grow out of it, others persist throughout their lives. Wool is often a favored item because it contains lanolin. It is a good idea to try a different type of bedding for such cats, although there is no guarantee that this will stop the habit.

Wool-sucking is common in Siamese cats. Cats should be discouraged from nibbling wool by removing woolen bedding and clothes.

Case history

Kim's cat, Winnie, was a young Siamese. Kim noticed that Winnie was becoming very interested in sucking and sometimes nibbling fabrics, in particular its bedding blankets and the family's woolen sweaters. Kim discussed the problem with the cat breeder, an expert in Siamese cats. She explained that Winnie had been weaned normally, so it was not comfort eating, but that as Siamese cats mature they are genetically inclined to develop a liking for wool. The breeder recommended that where possible, all woolen items should be removed so that the cat could not reach them. Later she could advise Kim if taste-aversion therapy needed to be used.

breakdown in
toilet training

Cats are very clean creatures by nature, but there may be times when your pet soils in the home for no apparent reason. It may have been that it was shut in somewhere in the house away from its litter pan while you were out and it had no other option. However, just the fact that the litter pan has already been used might in itself be sufficient cause for your cat to soil elsewhere.

The causes of spraying

There are several reasons a cat might spray in the home. You need to find the underlying reason for the spraying before you can cure the condition:

• Medical condition: If your cat is suffering from an illness such as cystitis or other kidney problem, this will cause it to urinate more frequently and it is more likely to soil around the home. If you suspect that your cat could be suffering from a medical problem of this type, you need to consult your veterinarian without delay.

Below: A cat living indoors must have constant access to a litter pan. Keep this in one place, so that your pet can find it easily in an emergency.

Above: Pet doors may allow unwanted visitors into your home, and it may not actually be your cat that is soiling here.

• Change in the environment: If there is no medical problem, then the most likely reason for spraying is a change in the cat's environment. Try to discover what could have triggered your pet's behavior. The cause is usually a major change such as moving house or introducing a baby or new pet.

• Sexual maturity: The most common reason for spraying in young cats, especially toms, is the onset of sexual maturity. Toms start to lay claim to their territory by spraying strong-smelling urine around the home. Although this is not as common in queens, they too will spray urine on occasions, once they are mature. Neutering usually overcomes this problem in the case of either sex.

If cats end up being shut indoors, and deprived of a litter pan they cannot be as fastidious about their toilet habits as usual.

• Unwelcome visitors: If you have a pet door that any cat can use, it may be that another cat has entered your home, unbeknown to you and may have sprayed here. Your cat may simply be reinforcing its claim to the house by responding in similar fashion. You may not be able to resolve this problem easily, although if you notice that your cat is apparently eating much more than usual, this is a good indication that another cat has entered the house. The simplest solution is to clean up thoroughly and then block

Below left: Clean the litter tray thoroughly if you suspect another cat has been using your cat's litter.

Below: Clean up and disinfect wet areas immediately.

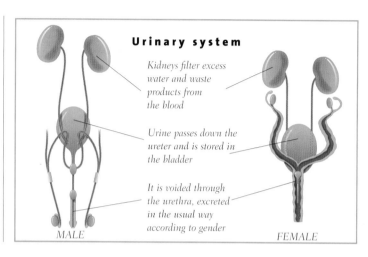

Urinary system

Kidneys filter excess water and waste products from the blood

Urine passes down the ureter and is stored in the bladder

It is voided through the urethra, excreted in the usual way according to gender

MALE   FEMALE

off the pet door for a week or so, to prevent any other cat from coming into your home. If this means keeping your cat indoors for longer than would otherwise be the case, provide a litter pan for your cat.

Stopping your cat spraying

Other changes in your cat's immediate environment can result in urine spraying. If your cat decides to use one particular place, in spite of your attempts to dissuade it, place some aluminum foil over the floor because cats dislike walking on this material. Alternatively, attach the aluminum foil to the wall of the area where the cat is tempted to spray. Cats will dislike the sound of their spray against aluminum foil.

You could also try placing your pet's food nearby for a short while, since cats rarely soil in areas close to their food. Alternatively, try keeping your cat out of that part of the house for a while.

Case history

The Ramseys had a problem with their cat, Morris. He had begun spraying in isolated areas around the house. Having taken him to the vet, his urine sample was tested, which showed he did not have a medical problem. After talking to the vet, the Ramseys realized that the problem was probably to do with stress. There had been builders and decorators around the house and his familiar scents and usual routine had been affected. To help solve the problem, they thoroughly cleaned the areas of wall where the cat had sprayed using a pet-odor neutralizer, and marked the areas with a pheromone spray that would discourage him from using the area again. As the house was restored to normal, they began to get Morris back into a routine that would reduce his stress levels and make him less inclined to spray.

when your cat disappears

It is very worrying when you let your cat outside, and it simply disappears. An instinctive reaction is to fear the worst—that your cat may have been badly injured or even killed in a traffic accident. Such fears often prove to be unfounded, fortunately.

Getting established

The risk of disappearances is usually greatest in the case of cats that are newcomers to an area, particularly where there are a number of other cats in the vicinity. This is because cats need to establish their own niches in the neighborhood, and if there is conflict, your cat may lose out and so disappears for a time.

Alternatively, if you have not moved very far, the cat may have gone back to its old haunts, so check with your former neighbors whether they have seen your pet recently. If so, bring your cat back to your new home and keep it confined indoors again for a further two to three weeks, until its urge to wander back to the locality of your previous home subsides.

Dealing with a bully

It is trickier if there is a neighborhood bully that is making your cat's life a misery in its new surroundings. The only answer will be to keep a powerful water pistol handy, so that you can squirt the aggressive cat whenever you see it in your yard. This may not impress its owner, but by so doing you should hopefully create a secure territory for your cat, especially if you have a magnetic pet door, affording your pet even greater security if it is challenged.

Male cats will not only fight over the neighborhood females, but they may also wander off over large distances, effectively disappearing for days at a time, before returning home bearing the scars of battle. The solution in this case

Some cats can be very aggressive toward newcomers in a neighborhood.

Securing a cat's identity

You can permanently identify your cat by
- ear tattoo
- implantable microchips.

Both have a central register or database listing. Ask at your clinic for more information.

Cats should be kept indoors during firework parties.

is to have the cat neutered so that it will be far less likely to behave in this way in the future.

Sources of fright

Yet it is not just fights with others of their kind that may cause cats to disappear. Basically, anything that frightens them can have this effect, ranging from thunder to fireworks, so always try to plan ahead and bring your cat indoors before it becomes frightened and disappears. Cats often retreat into dark, confined spaces when they feel under threat, so if your cat does vanish, it is worthwhile looking carefully in sheds or garages. Since they can easily become shut in such

Cats often retreat to somewhere they can be alone if they are sick or injured. You need to check all outside sheds.

buildings unnoticed, ask your neighbors to check in their sheds as well. You may then need to begin a wider search.

Cats may also vanish when they feel unwell, so if you suspect that your cat could be sick, do not allow it outside, but keep it confined with a litter pan. Otherwise, you may not be able to give vital medicine to ensure your pet's recovery.

Treatment Tips
If your cat is missing

- Don't panic. Search your house and yard thoroughly first, including all possible hiding places.
- Ask the immediate neighbors to check your cat is not locked into their sheds or garages.
- Tell people you know. Put up notices locally. Describe the cat, give your details, and offer a reward for its return.

- Inform the local cat shelters and veterinary practices.
- Tell the police. Let them know if you suspect theft (if it is a valuable pedigree cat).
- Ask the local street cleaner if you think your cat may have been knocked over.
- Do not give up hope. Cats can be missing for long periods, only to return acting as if nothing has happened.

aggression

toward people

Some cats are instinctively more friendly toward people than others. This partly depends on their experiences early in life. Kittens that missed out on the socialization period (see pages 128–129) are likely to be more withdrawn and quite unfriendly toward people. Sometimes, however, a cat of this type may form a close bond with one person, and yet remain very shy with everyone else. Nervous cats will often strike out if they are cornered in any way, and you may need to restrain them by the scruff of the neck to avoid being bitten.

Inflicting wounds

Cats often become aggressive if they are in pain, and this can be sufficient to make even a normally docile cat strike out with its claws or jaws. Take extra care if you are handling your cat when it is in this state, or you could end up being hurt.

• Bites: Cats have a very unpleasant bacterial flora in their mouths, which means that a cat bite is likely to turn septic. The wound must be cleaned thoroughly; and a germicidal ointment used, particularly if the long, narrow, canine teeth have penetrated the skin. If the injury starts to show signs of inflammation, you may need to seek medical help, especially if you have not had a tetanus vaccine within the last few years.

• Scratches: Scratches from the claws must also be carefully cleaned, and they are likely to throb for some time afterward.

Above: Cats can be very friendly towards people they know well and rub against them with their scent glands. The friendliness of individual cats can depend on their early experiences as kittens.

Wise precautions

• Rabies: Whenever the character of a cat changes dramatically, bear in mind the slight possibility of rabies. This of course depends on where you are in the world, since islands such as Britain, Ireland, Australia, and Hawaii, among others, are presently free of this deadly viral disease. Should there be the slightest risk that your cat could be infected by rabies, aim to keep it confined and seek the advice of a vet without delay. This infection represents a serious, even fatal, threat to human health and because it is found within wildlife populations, cats that hunt can become infected by their prey. In areas where rabies is endemic, where at all possible, cats should always be vaccinated against this virus.

Other displays of aggression

• Play aggression: Kittens can sometimes bite unintentionally if they are allowed or encouraged to play roughly. If a kitten is aggressive, the best way to treat it is to ignore it for a few minutes. It will soon learn to be less aggressive.

• Feeding: Feeding can sometimes provoke displays of aggression, particularly if you pat your cat on its head as you give the food. The cat may become impatient and bite in anticipation of having its food, so simply do not pet your cat at this point. It will still retain aggressive instincts just before it eats, in the same way that a wildcat hunts for food and only relaxes after it has made its kill and eaten.

Treatment Tips

Ways of controlling aggression

EARLY LEARNING

In the early weeks, situations that lead to aggressive behavior in a kitten should be discouraged.

AVERSION THERAPY

If a cat associates its aggressive behavior with something unpleasant happening, this can help to change its behavior.

MEDICAL ADVICE

Some aggressive conditions can be treated with drugs. There may be physical cause of the aggression.

Right: A cat can inflict painful scratches with its sharp claws, so be aware of mood changes from affection to aggression.

Top: A Siamese in an aggressive posture.

Above: Cats dislike being disturbed when feeding.

Left: Cats will leap up aggressively if teased with toys.

aggression

toward other cats

Fighting among cats is usually for territorial reasons, although in many cases such disputes are settled before there is any serious display of violence. If neither cat backs down, however, then a fight will occur. Encounters of this type are brief, violent affairs, with cats using both their claws and teeth in a bid to overcome the opponent. The weaker individual will soon seek the opportunity to break away, briefly pursued by the victor. The fight itself will be accompanied by loud shrieks of growing intensity uttered by the combatants, which are intended to intimidate each other.

1. Left: The tabby cat is behaving aggressively here, challenging the somewhat impassive white cat by stalking it.

2. Right: It is not just body language that cats use to communicate aggression. Cats will hiss and call menacingly as well.

3. Right: In this instance, the tabby cat has decided to back off. Unfortunately, if you have two cats that do not agree, then persistent challenges of this type are likely to occur.

Battle scars

In spite of the ferocity of such encounters, cats rarely inflict serious injury on each other. Their dense coats provide a barrier against claws, although their eyes are vulnerable to being scratched. Some chunks of fur are likely to be pulled out, but these soon regrow. Their ears may sometimes be torn, however, and this can result in permanent scarring.

Abscesses

The most common injury after a fight will not be immediately apparent in most cases, but within a couple of days a bite wound to the head is likely to give rise to an abscess—a swelling that can grow alarmingly in size. It needs to be bathed with salt water to encourage it to burst, and if you look carefully, you may just be able to detect the toothmarks of the other cat on the stretched skin. An abscess of this type can make a cat feel seriously unwell, depressing its appetite and overall level of activity. Once the abscess ruptures, however, your cat should start to feel better,

although antibiotics may be needed to assist its recovery. There is a more sinister risk attached to fights of this type, however, and the Feline AIDS virus is just one infection that can be spread between cats in this way. Neutering a male cat should lessen its likelihood of being involved in conflicts of this type.

Fighting tom

Sometimes, there can be one very aggressive tom in the neighborhood, which attacks all other cats that are allowed outside. The best solution may be to have a discreet word with its owner (unless of course the cat is feral) explaining that the cat is causing a lot of suffering to others in the area, in the hope of arranging for this tom to be neutered and hopefully restoring feline harmony.

Cats can end up having to defend territories not just against other domestics, but also feral cats.

Recurrent bouts of fighting between toms are common, and your cat can suffer repeated injuries. Every encounter has risks attached to it, so as a further precaution it is a good idea to ensure that your cat is kept in at night, when conflicts of this type are most likely to arise.

Case history

Mat's cat, a neutered tabby named Racer was being attacked by a tom cat in his own backyard. On several occasions, Mat had to take Racer to the vet because of bite wounds inflicted by the tom. Although Racer could defend himself, he was no match for the tomcat. Nobody appeared to own the cat and Mat accepted that it may be a feral cat from a farm a short distance away. The tomcat was patrolling a territory in which no cat could be safe. With the help of a local organization, a humane trap was set for the feral cat and it was caught one night as it entered the trap in search of food prepared for it. The cat was transported safely in a covered cage to the clinic, where it had been arranged that the feral would be neutered, ear-tipped for identification, and checked for disease. Later that day, the altered male cat was released back into its territory.

moving home
with your cat

In all the planning surrounding a move, it is important not to overlook your pet's needs. Cats are sensitive creatures and will soon realize that changes are afoot when you start packing up. It is probably a good idea, particularly if you are moving quite a long distance, to arrange to transfer your cat to a boarding establishment near your new home a few days before you move. You can then be assured that your cat will be safe. With the disturbance of moving out of a home, a cat might run off and disappear. This is not only very worrying for the owners but could also create serious logistical problems and the cat may end up a stray.

Preparing the new environment

While your cat is being boarded, you can make the necessary preparations to help it settle down well in its new home. It is definitely not a good idea to introduce a cat to new surroundings where building work is underway, particularly since you will need to keep it confined in the house to stop it from straying. The noise, fumes, and the presence of strangers coming in and out will all prove stressful for your pet. It may resort to creeping into places where it might end up being trapped, retreating beneath raised floorboards, for example, and hiding here when these are relaid.

Even if you are not having major structural works carried out in your new home, a cat can easily brush against wet paintwork and get paint on its coat. Should this happen, it is important to remove the paint from the fur, otherwise the cat will lick it off as it grooms itself and make itself sick. If necessary, you will have to rinse the coat or even give your cat a bath.

Do not overlook your cat's needs when you are planning a move. A stay at a boarding establishment for your pet is often the best solution while you are packing up.

Far left: Clean the carpets in a new home to remove scents of previous occupants.

Left: At first, you may want to exercise your cat on a leash until it can be allowed to roam.

Below: Cats sometimes return to the old home if this is nearby.

Home from home

One of the most important things you need to do to make your cat feel at home in its new environment is to arrange to have all the carpeting cleaned professionally. This will remove the scent of any previous feline resident, which may otherwise be distressing to your pet.

Many owners blame their cat for a breakdown in toilet training in the period immediately following a move. The cat is usually just trying to mask out the scent of the previous occupant and lay claim to its new territory. When you transfer your cat to its new home,

It will take several weeks for your cat to accept the move to a new home and settle down here.

be sure to have a litter tray available, even if previously your cat has been allowed to wander freely outdoors. This is important because your cat will need to be kept permanently inside for at least two weeks so that it comes to accept your new home as the center of its territory. Your cat may live in just one room for a while before it explores the rest of the house, especially if you are trying to organize yourselves and your furniture in different rooms. Give your cat plenty of reassurance in its new home.

These measures should stop a cat from trying to return to its former haunts. Remember to change the identification tag on its collar to the new address, just in case your cat is tempted to wander off when it goes outside. If your cat allows it, a harness can also be useful at first for walking the cat around its new territory.

Travel with cats

A cat on a long journey needs
- a secure, well-ventilated cat carrier
- a litter pan and litter
- a familiar blanket or bedding
- a favorite toy
- a drinking dish and water container
- a sedative (if advised by the veterinarian).

eating problems
and loss of appetite

Cats can be quite fussy about their food and may not take readily to changing from one brand of food to another. This is why it is important to get them used to eating different types of food from an early age, rather than relying on one type of food from kittenhood onwards. An unexpected and sudden loss of appetite can be a sign of illness (also see pages 130–131), but it may also simply mean that your cat has found another source of food in the neighborhood, which it prefers. Cats can be very fickle, and you may be able to overcome the problem by switching from dry food to canned food (see also pages 80–81), which most cats prefer. If this is still ignored, further investigation may be needed.

Establishing a routine

Cats living wild do not eat every day, nor as a rule will they scavenge like dogs. They prefer fresh food, so if a cat is faced with canned food that has dried up in its bowl, it will probably ignore it.

In the wild, cats eat their prey soon after killing it, so they prefer warm food. A cat that is a fussy eater is less likely to eat food straight from the refrigerator, so it is best to take the food out about 15–20 minutes before it is fed.

Above: Use a can cover to prevent the cat's food from being tainted by other foods in the refrigerator.

Left: Cats need a quiet environment in which to eat. If they are upset they will ignore their food, although this is more likely to be a sign of sickness.

Loss of appetite

Cats may lose their appetites for short periods as the result for a number of reasons including
• being badly frightened
• moving house
• a change in circumstances
• the loss of an owner
• depression
• loud noises such as fireworks or a thunderstorm.

This will allow the food to come to room temperature in the cat's bowl, or you can gently warm the food to meet your cat's needs.

It will also help to overcome feeding problems later in life if you only allow your pet access to its food for a set amount of time. Your cat will soon develop the routine of eating as soon as it is fed, rather than picking at its food, going away, and then returning to eat a little more (this type of behavior can also be a sign that the cat has a furball in its stomach—the obstruction allows the cat to eat only in small quantities, rather than eating the whole meal in a single sitting.)

Furballs

Furballs are most likely to afflict longhaired cats when they are molting, so grooming at this stage to remove the shed fur from the coat is particularly important.

A furball can cause loss of appetite in longhaired cats by partly filling the stomach, leaving less space for food.

There are now special diets available that help to prevent the accumulation of furballs, although a laxative suitable for a cat should assist the passage of what is a solid mass of fur out of the stomach.

Case history

Tess, the cat belonging to Mrs. Jenkins, had lost interest in life. She had stopped grooming and was not eating her food. Mrs. Jenkins had taken her to the veterinarian and there did not seem to be a medical problem. She could only guess that Tess had been affected by her youngest daughter, Rona, recently leaving home, because they had been very close. The vet suggested that Tess was depressed and that she needed lots of special care and attention. She should be helped with grooming and most important, tempted to eat food again. Mrs. Jenkins should feed her by hand if necessary. It would be best if Tess could be gently nursed back to her normal self. If she did not improve, the veterinarian could prescribe antidepressant drugs that would help Tess.

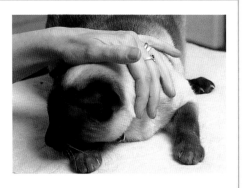

new relationships
and our pets

When embarking on a new relationship, pets are unlikely to be uppermost in your mind—but they can cause some difficulties. One of the most difficult situations is when one partner is allergic to the other partner's cat, suffering runny eyes and nose, and possibly even wheezing.

Allergic reactions

Research to produce a desensitizing injection is ongoing, but for many couples in this predicament there is no easy solution. Keeping the cat confined to one place in the

Left: Before long, a cat will settle well in a home with a new person, although usually, your pet will still come instinctively to you first.

Below: Get your new partner involved with your cat.

house, away from the bedroom and living room, provides some relief for the sufferer, and grooming outside helps to lessen the risk of skin particles and hair being deposited in the home. A vacuum cleaner that is specially adapted for cleaning up after pets can also help. Breeds with a relatively sparse covering of hair, such as the Devon Rex and Sphynx, are said to be less likely to produce an allergic response than longhaired breeds such as the Persian, but this depends very much on the individual person.

Above left: Allergies to cats are quite common, especially with longhaired cats such as the Maine Coon, shown here, or other cats such as Persians.

Nervous of cats

Not everyone likes cats, however, and if your new partner is perhaps a bit nervous of a cat, this too can cause problems, especially since your cat may feel threatened by the presence of an apparent stranger in the home. You need to persuade your partner to become involved in caring for the cat, perhaps always feeding your pet in the morning, for example, and gradually a bond should build up between them. Even so, the likelihood is that your cat will continue to feel a greater bond with you, especially if it has grown up in your company since kittenhood.

It can be harder to persuade your new partner's cat to become friendly with your cat. Do not attempt to rush this process.

Feline introductions

A particularly tricky situation is when both you and your partner have cats, who have not met until you set up home together. The likelihood of a relatively harmonious introduction may be greater if you are setting up a new home together, rather than if one of you is moving in with the other.

Solutions

The best solution is to put both cats in a boarding establishment first. Here they can be introduced to each other on neutral territory, possibly even sharing a unit, although you should be guided by the advice of the owner. Bringing them both back home together will lessen the likelihood of conflict. They will need to be kept in to prevent them from straying.

Other considerations

• Litter pans: Provide each cat with a separate litter pan.
• Feeding: Be sure to feed the cats separately, since the risk of outbreaks of aggression is dramatically increased when cats are being fed.
• Toilet training: You may still encounter some breakdown in toilet training, but this phase should pass quite rapidly when the cats have settled down.

Within a few weeks, most cats living together in this way will at least be studiously ignoring each other rather than being persistently aggressive.

Treatment Tips
Allergic reactions to cats

Many more people are allergic to cats than to dogs. They are not always allergic to cat hair, but more often the dead skin, or dander, of a cat. They may also be allergic to the protein found in a cat's saliva, so a cat scratch can cause an allergic reaction if there is saliva on the paws.

SKIN
Keep a cat's skin in good condition to reduce dander and saliva that is licked onto the coat. Bathing a cat, or rubbing a cat several times a day with a damp cloth or sponge, may help.

COAT
Brush the coat outside so the dander does not settle indoors.

CLAWS
Cut the claws outside so the nails are not lying around indoors.

the introduction
of a baby

Once settled into a routine, cats do not take readily to change, especially as they grow older. It is therefore important to minimize alterations to their lifestyle as much as possible, keeping in particular to regular mealtimes. However, one of the most significant changes that can occur in a family, which totally alters the usual routine is the birth of a baby.

Care in pregnancy

The need for good hygiene in cat care becomes increasingly important, especially during pregnancy:

• Taxoplasma: There is a slight risk posed by *Toxoplasma gonadii* (also see pages 64–65) which may be passed out of the cat's body in its feces. It could present a serious hazard to a pregnant woman who has not encountered this parasite earlier in life because it can cross the placenta and cause abortion. In addition to wearing gloves when changing the contents of a cat's litter pan, gloves should be worn when gardening, since cat feces are frequently buried in soil.

• Worms: Following your vet's advice, it is important to eliminate the risk of any parasitic worms that might also be transmitted to people.

The cat's sleeping arrangements

It is not a good idea to allow a cat to sleep in your bedroom, partly because of the risk that it will bring fleas here, but particularly if you will be introducing a baby. After the baby's birth, your cat should not be allowed in

Never leave a cat and young baby on their own together in a room. They should always be supervised.

the bedroom and it may react badly as a result. You are likely to find that it does not settle well, especially at night, and may meow consistently when confined elsewhere in the home.

If your cat does this, the best thing is to ignore it completely, or your cat will soon learn that its behavior will gain your attention whenever it wants something.

Settling the cat

You can help to settle a cat down in a new part of the home by preparing everything for it in advance. If you play with the cat and then feed it at night, it should be ready to settle down on its own. Check the

Useful lessons

When children are old enough, try and teach them

• not to disturb a sleeping cat

• to play and move carefully near a cat

• not to make sudden loud noises near a cat

• how to pick up a cat properly

• how to care for a cat properly.

temperature of the cat's room—if it is likely to be much colder here, you may want to provide a thin pad heater under the bedding, which gives off gentle warmth.

Right: Be sure that your baby cannot inadvertently hurt your cat, which may otherwise react by biting or scratching.

Baby care

When the baby arrives, your cat will be curious about the noisy newcomer, but it will probably lose interest fairly soon. Let your cat get accustomed to the new smells. But it is important not to allow your cat into the bedroom with a young baby left on its own. Also, place a special cover over the crib, to dissuade the cat from climbing in alongside the baby, attracted by the baby's warmth or the covers. There are reports of cats accidentally suffocating babies under these

Right: If you have a toddler in the home, provide your cat with a hooded litter pan.

Left: Although your attention will be with a young child, make sure the cat does not feel neglected.

circumstances, so it is potentially very dangerous. As a further safety measure in the home, it may also be more hygienic to use hooded litter pans with a cat-flap entrance when a baby starts crawling.

Cat care

Your attention will be with the baby. Set aside some time to spend with your cat to make up for changes in its lifestyle and help it not to feel neglected. Otherwise, the cat may start spraying to cover up the scent of the baby or wander off in search of another home.

Once a baby begins to be aware of the cat, teach it to treat the cat with care. The baby should be taught not to pull its tail or disturb the cat when it is sleeping.

winning the trust
of a nervous cat

Cats that have been neglected or abused, especially during kittenhood, will tend to be nervous in later life and it can often be very difficult to win back their trust. Sometimes, keeping a cat of this type in the company of another, bolder individual may help to regain its confidence, although you need to ensure that it is not being bullied, which of course will worsen the situation.

Winning back trust

A cat who is nervous will tend to move more slowly and deliberately than usual, especially when in open spaces, such as crossing a floor, for example. It will prefer to sit in parts of the room where it has a good view of what is going on, but without being conspicuous. The worst thing that you can do under these circumstances is to tower above the cat, whether to pick it up or make a fuss of it. You need to do the following:

• Crouch or lie down next to the cat, to persuade it that you represent no threat.

• Speak softly to help give the cat confidence.

Cats are usually nervous because of something that happened in the past.

Natural remedies

These remedies can all be used to treat situations caused by fear
• rock rose
• mimulus
• rescue remedy
• holly.
Refer to a Bach Flower Remedy therapist for advice and treatment.

• Encourage the cat to play, perhaps by dragging a piece of thick rope along for it to pounce on.

Inherent problems

There is no quick solution when dealing with a nervous cat, although it will be easier if you can identify why it reacts in this way. If it is a general problem the likelihood is that your cat will never become as friendly as

It can be a slow process winning back the trust of a nervous cat, but it can be achieved successfully with patience. Your cat will gradually learn to trust you.

Playing with your cat offers a good way of winning its trust. Never try to rush things however—this process takes time.

• Breed characteristics: Breed differences can be significant as well. The Bengal, for example, is less well-domesticated than other breeds, because of crossings carried out with wild Asian leopard cats, which underlie its ancestry. Although breeders have concentrated on ensuring a sound temperament in this breed, some Bengal cats do tend to be more nervous than others by nature.

• Medical history: If you have acquired a cat that appears to be very nervous of people, it may be worthwhile having it checked out by your veterinarian because this may give some indication of why it is nervous. For instance, it could reveal injuries that have now healed, such as fracture. There is also always the possibility that your cat might have been peppered with airgun pellets that are still lodged in its body. These will only show up on an X-ray.

one that has been raised in a secure home from kittenhood. Consider the following in relation to your cat:

• Bloodline: With purebred cats, nervousness can be more of a problem in certain bloodlines than others, so it pays to check on this aspect before purchasing a kitten.

Although you will not want to rely on keeping your cat sedated because of its nervous nature, you may decide to use soothing herbal or homeopathic treatments for this purpose. Bach Flower Remedies have also become popular among cat owners to overcome nervousness in their pets.

Case history

Joy's cat, Pluto, was a rescue cat who was very nervous of going outside. Joy was not sure what caused the stress, but Pluto had probably been a victim of a bullying cat in the past. Joy had an enclosed and safe backyard, so she was sure that Pluto would not be disturbed and frightened by other cats in his new home. To deal with his nervousness, Joy investigated some herbal remedies. Recommended doses of valerian or skullcap would help Pluto to be less fearful about stepping outside and boost his confidence. In order to encourage him to go past the back door, Joy started to move his food bowl nearer and nearer to the door at mealtimes. Pluto would build up confidence about going into the backyard. Along with plenty of encouragement and patience, an outdoor bowl would probably help Pluto to make that final step outside.

when affection turns to

aggression

Some cats appear to behave in a very disturbing way, being highly affectionate one moment and then suddenly leaping up and scratching or even biting without warning. This can be especially upsetting for children, who are not aware of the risk of this sudden switch in personality and can suffer a painful injury as a result. Children should be taught to read the signs of when a cat has had enough, and take particular care in stroking the underside of a cat.

Lightning reactions

A reaction is often triggered when you stroke the cat's underparts. When a cat rolls over onto its back, it is at its most vulnerable. If it suddenly feels threatened, it will lash out with its paws, particularly toward a person whom it does not trust as much as its owner. Its body language changes rapidly from being relaxed and submissive to displaying signs of overt aggression, and mounting what would in feline terms be perceived as a challenge.

Submissive and aggressive behavior

Such behavior can be related directly to the way that cats interact with each other. When you start stroking a cat, it adopts a submissive posture, with its head low upon its shoulders and its ears flattened. If the cat were threatened by

This is a submissive posture, which reveals that your cat trusts you not to hurt it. But watch for sudden mood changes.

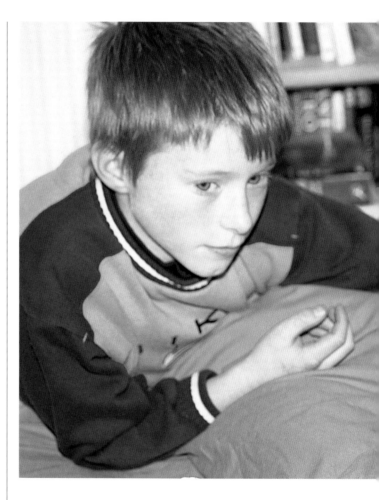

an aggressor and this failed to deter it, it would apparently continue its submissive behavior by rolling over on to its back. But in this position, the cat will be looking to lash out with its paws rather than its jaws, to catch the aggressor off balance and give itself the opportunity to escape.

Behavioral instincts

While a cat that is being stroked in this way is obviously not under threat, its behavioral instincts suggest that it could be, particularly if a hand is raised near its head. The cat is confused about what is happening, and reacts

Left: Children need to be shown how to handle cats so that they do not hurt them, and to appreciate that their pets like to sleep rather than play all day.

Right: Picking up a cat incorrectly can easily lead to your being scratched, if it struggles.

instinctively with an aggressive response. Once you have raised your hand in pain, having been scratched, the cat may dart off a short distance away and sits there swishing its tail angrily from side to side. It may then start to groom itself determinedly, engaging in what is described as a displacement activity, being unsure of what it has done.

Solutions

There is no point in scolding your cat for this. In fact, this is a difficult behavioral problem to address successfully. The best solution may simply be to avoid stroking your cat's underparts—or remove your hand before any sign of aggression begins. Wearing a leather glove and pinning your cat down if it tries to behave in this way is likely to be counterproductive, because it will simply scare your pet. Provided that you are aware of this particular problem and avoid it, it will not impact greatly on your relationship with your cat.

Cats enjoy being stroked in many ways, such as being rubbed and tickled under the chin. Over the course of time, you may find that your cat relaxes more with you, allowing you to stroke it gently on its underparts, when it chooses, and without always setting off an aggressive reaction.

Treatment Tips
Stroking a cat

There are known benefits to humans of stroking a cat. To control aggression in your cat, try the following

- pet your cat only for a short period of time
- use single strokes, imitating a mother's tongue
- avoid stroking the parts of the body that cause aggression.

---

behavioral changes
in old age

Cats do not show the obvious signs of aging, such as graying of the coat, but as they grow older you are likely to notice that their level of activity slow downs. They will sleep for longer and are more reluctant to go outside, particularly when the weather is bad.

Physical characteristics of old age

• Eyesight: Eyesight becomes less acute as a cat gets older because the rods and cones lose their elasticity. You may notice a blue-gray clouding of the eyes.

• Hearing: Hearing declines, making your cat less responsive as it gets older.

• Body: The coat may become duller. You will probably notice slackening of the skin and more prominent hips.

• Joints and limbs: Legs become less agile showing stiffness especially when it gets up first thing in the morning.

• Teeth: The teeth can deteriorate, and there may be a build-up of tartar, which can lead to gum inflammation and gingivitis.

• Claws: Claws can become overgrown (see pages 102–103) if an elderly cat stops scratching.

• Body systems: Chemical and hormone responses lessen and brain function slows. Lungs and circulatory system become less efficient. Despite these general physical changes, all cats are individuals and your cat may be affected by any of

Cats tend to become less active by nature as they grow older. They like routine and home comforts, and dislike change.

them to a greater or lesser extent. An elderly cat can lead a healthy life until very old age.

Care of an elderly cat

You may need to pay more attention to the following areas as your cat becomes older:

It is quite usual for older cats to want to sleep for long periods, and this is simply a part of old age.

Extra help for an elderly cat

• comb regularly
• provide with a warm bed
• supply extra litter pans
• raise the level of food and water bowls
• feed a high-protein diet
• keep claws trimmed
• keep teeth clean
• keep to a routine
• have regular checks at the clinic.

• Diet: Some older cats may have a problem with chewing their food. It may be a good idea to change to a soft, moist diet or a special diet recommended by the veterinarian.

• Grooming: Grooming can become more difficult for an elderly cat, so be prepared to help out, by wiping around the eyes, for example, as well as combing the coat. Check the claws too, because these can become overgrown, making walking both difficult and painful.

• Litter pan: A cat may neglect the litter pan in its later years because it may not be able to move so easily and it may need to urinate more than usual. A low-sided pan may be required for easier access.

• Sleeping arrangements: Your cat may find it more comfortable to sleep on a bean bag rather than in a cat bed where it has to curl up. It may no longer find it as comfortable sleeping on your lap.

Problems of an elderly cat

• Diabetes mellitus (sugar diabetes): This is caused by a decrease in the hormone insulin produced by the cat's body. It is more common in overweight cats, who become very thirsty. It may need to be controlled by a strict diet to lose weight, or by a daily dose of insulin.

Grooming can be more problematic in old age, partly because the cat's body is not as supple as it was. In addition, since the claws may not be worn down as much, they may curl around at their tips.

Left: Gently clean the corners of the eyes if these appear dirty.

Below: Accidents may happen around the home. It could be that the sides of the litter pan are too high, making it difficult for your cat to climb over them.

• Thyroid problems: An overactive thyroid gland will cause an elderly cat to be overactive. It may be constantly on the move, very thirsty, and demanding food. Although the cat may eat more than usual, it will not gain weight. The condition can be helped by medication or surgery. Left untreated it could cause the heart to fail under the increased strain. Underactivity of the thyroid can cause bad-temperedness and aggressiveness.

• Kidney problems: A common problem of old age is weight loss, which is often linked with chronic kidney failure. Kidney problems affect all cats as they grow older, to a greater or lesser extent. Only when about 80% of the kidney tissue is damaged, however, will serious signs of illness become apparent. You may find that a cat drinks a lot more fluid. You must allow your cat to drink as it wishes, or you could endanger its life. Although it may not be possible to cure a kidney condition, it can be stabilized by dietary and other means, so that your cat can maintain a good quality of life for many months, if not years.

when to seek help
for your cat

If you have not owned a cat before, it is sometimes difficult to know whether your pet is behaving as it should, or if it is developing a behavioral problem. In most cases, there will be nothing to worry about, and kittens especially are full of energy and may behave in unusual ways before settling down. Early indicators of a problem are harder to detect at this age, therefore, compared with an older cat that has already established a behavioral pattern.

Assessing the problem

It is important to be able to identify a behavioral problem. It can involve:
• Repetitive patterns of behaviour: An example of this is repeated grooming, leading to hair loss or alopecia.
On the other hand, a cat that learns to beg to attract its owner's attention is not necessarily suffering from a behavioral problem despite behaving in an unusual way for a cat. Do not ignore the role that you may play in the development of such practices.

Repetitive grooming can be a behavioral problem that develops over a period of time.

• Learned undesirable practices: It may seem cute to have a cat begging for food but if you start to reward it, your pet will soon behave persistently in this way. In this instance the practice may be fine. On the other hand, there can be other cases when, by your actions, you reinforce an undesirable behavioral trait.

You may not even be aware of what is happening, but if you have a cat that meows to go out and you respond by letting it out immediately, it will soon start behaving consistently in this fashion, calling loudly and persistently until you respond to its demands.

Medical or behavioral?

It may not always be apparent whether your cat has a behavioral problem or an underlying medical condition if, for example, it suddenly starts urinating randomly around the home. A number of factors, such as its age and whether it is neutered, will give some likely indicators as to the source of the problem.

Encouraging your cat to eat from your hand may be necessary if it is unwell, but long term, it could discourage the cat from eating on its own.

Right: Cats will adapt their behavior for rewards, just like dogs. Once given a tasty mouthful in return for begging, they will repeat this action in the future.

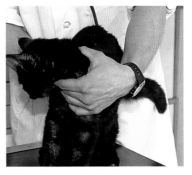

Should a medical problem be ruled out, then your vet may still be able to advise you, or refer you to a behaviorist specializing in feline problems.

It is generally easier to rule out medical problems first, so a veterinary investigation should be carried out initially. Once this has been completed, any possible underlying behavioral causes can be examined in detail.

This approach is generally favored, because a medical problem, such as urinating over carpets indoors as the result of a kidney infection, can also lead to a change in the cat's regular pattern of behavior. It returns to this spot because it has scent-marked here previously and wishes to reinforce the scent as a territorial marker, for behavioral reasons. In such cases, once the medical condition has been identified and treated accordingly, then it should be possible to deal separately with the behavioral problem. Remember that, in many cases, what seem to us to be behavioral problems actually reflect aspects of the natural behavior of wildcats, which are no longer considered appropriate within domestic surroundings.

Above: If you are worried about your cat's behavior, arrange to see your veterinarian first, to find out if there is an underlying medical cause for the problem.

Case history

Ujai was concerned about his elderly cat, Kookie. Kookie was a 15-year-old male who had suddenly become irritable. Little events upset him, even if it was just an unusual happening at home or a change in the routine. Being late with a meal would bring on an aggressive display, sometimes even biting Ujai on the hand, which Ujai had never experienced from Kookie before. Ujai was concerned about Kookie and took him to the clinic. The veterinarian examined the cat and suggested that symptoms of old age including arthritis and sore gums were responsible for the change in behavior. When cats are in pain, they show their anger through aggression. The veterinarian could treat the medical condition, which in turn would affect the behavior of the cat in a positive way.

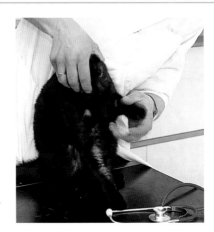

contacting
a pet behaviorist

A good reason for approaching your veterinarian first, rather than seeking out a pet behaviorist directly, is that if you are referred by a veterinarian, the fees may well be recoverable under a pet insurance policy. If you go directly to a behaviorist, then you are likely to have to pay the fees yourself, even if you have insurance cover for your cat.

Finding the right behaviorist

A further practical reason for this approach is that the veterinarian and pet behaviorist may need to work closely together. It is important that you see the person who is in the best position to help you with your cat's problem. As in all fields, some behaviorists tend to specialize in cats more than other pets, for example, or in certain types of disorders, and your veterinarian will be able to advise you accordingly.

Once it has been decided that your cat needs to see a behaviorist, it is likely that you may have to wait a while, because in some countries, there are relatively few behaviorists. You may need to be prepared to take your cat some distance for a consultation, although generally behaviorists have clinics that are easily accessible for clients. Often, these are organized on the premises of a veterinarian, where local clients can bring their pets.

Alternatively, you may be asked to take your cat to the behaviorist's own consulting rooms, although only rarely will a cat be admitted here for a stay for observation.

Above: In some cases, the behaviorist may prefer to see you with your cat in your home surroundings, since this can sometimes help to reveal much about the problem.

Increasing numbers of educational institutes offer animal behavior courses.

Left: You cannot usually expect immediate results from behavioral therapy.

The extent of the problem and how you follow the advice are important in determining the outcome.

Sometimes, especially with a particularly difficult case, the behaviorist may prefer to arrange a visit to your home. The behaviorist will see you, your family and your cat together in the home environment. This can sometimes give a vital insight into the cause of the problem.

Following advice

Although you clearly need to seek help for your pet without delay, it is not a good idea to arrange a behavioral consultation just before going away on vacation, for example, or moving home. You will not be able to put the behaviorist's advice into practice for any length of time under these circumstances and, more significantly, your cat is likely to be upset by the change in its environment. The best results are likely to be achieved when you are able to give your pet adequate time and attention, in a stable situation where it has a normal routine.

Getting results

When it comes to addressing behavioral problems, there is no magic formula in the shape of a tablet that can be popped into your cat's mouth or food. It is important to remember that what is ultimately likely to determine whether the counselor's recommendations will be successful is the amount of time and effort you are prepared to invest in following the advice you receive.

Treatment Tips

The most common behavioral problems in cats are

• Learned aggression
Unwanted scratching may be caused by stress or fear.

• Elimination behavior
Spraying is especially common in houses with more than one cat.

working to solve
a pet's problem

One of the most important aspects of a successful consultation with a behaviorist is often careful preparation on the part of the owner. Information can be vital to isolate the cause of the problem, helping it to be addressed successfully. It is therefore a good idea to write down as much information as possible in note form, in a diary-type format, allowing you to trace the development of the problem in chronological order as far as possible.

Keeping a "problem" diary

By doing this at home, you can check dates quite easily on a calendar and confirm information with other members of the family as necessary, to be sure that you have a detailed and accurate statement of how the problem has developed. You may want to overlay this with any changes that occur in family life, such as going on vacation, starting a new job,

acquiring a new puppy or similar events, which could in some way be involved in the development of the cat's abnormal behavior. It may also be helpful if you have some video footage of your cat behaving abnormally, since this can help the behaviorist to analyze the severity of the disorder in some cases.

Always act as soon as you suspect something is amiss. This is likely to make it much easier to resolve the problem.

Addressing the problem

Each behaviorist has a slightly different way of working; occasionally he or she will find it helpful to see all members of the family, especially in cases where a cat behaves aggressively toward one person in the household, but not another. When it comes to proposing what can be done, do not hesitate to ask for clarification if you are at all unsure of what you and other family members need to do to try and resolve the situation.

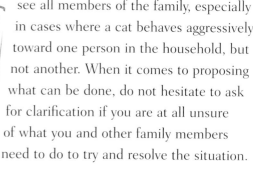

Accurate recording will give a behaviorist valuable insight into your cat's problem. Notes, dates, and even videos of your cat's actions and behavior can all be useful for this purpose.

If you are in any doubt about the treatment, write out what is required, because it can be quite easy to forget important details, and you can also raise any queries that come to mind while you are writing down the behaviorist's recommendations.

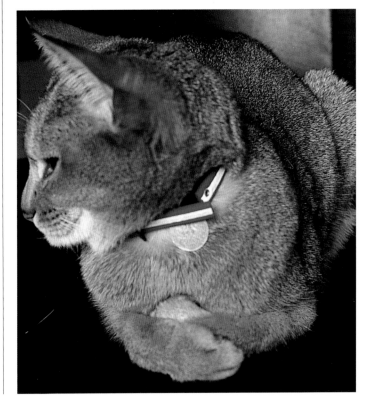

Above: In certain cases, medication may be helpful for your cat, at least at the outset, before the problem is resolved.

Giving treatment

In the first instance, it may be necessary to use a combination of medical treatment and environmental changes to deal with the problem. Then, once the condition starts to improve, there will be less reliance on medication, and ultimately it should be possible to phase this out entirely.

In some cases, your cat should respond rapidly when working to a plan recommended by a pet behaviorist, but just as with medical treatment, you will need to continue the treatment to obtain the best results. Keep a watch on your cat's behavior for any signs that it could be lapsing back into its former ways, since once the cause has been identified, you should be able to prevent further episodes by acting quickly. Do not expect immediate, lasting results because it will take time to effect a complete transformation in your cat's habits. However, with patience, lasting improvements will occur in time.

Below: Individual behavioral problems can be complex and need to be dealt with accordingly.

Treatment Tips

Controlling behavior

These practices are known to work in the majority of cases

• avoid encouraging any activity that leads to aggressive behavior
• try to 'unlearn' or eliminate undesirable behavior
• use aversion therapy if other remedies do not work
• consider the use of prescribed drugs to control aggressive behavior
• unless required for breeding, always neuter males and females from an early age
• treat physical pain caused by a cat's medical condition
• never use an unrelated punishment or punish after the event.

glossary

Abscess A painful swelling of pus under a cat's skin. It is usually the result of a cat fight, caused when bacteria invades a wound. When the abscess bursts, the matter will discharge.

Aversion therapy A means of treating an undesirable behavioral trait, by persuading the cat that such behavior results in an unpleasant experience.

Banding The pattern of alternating light and dark rings of fur seen on the tail of tabby cats, or on individual hairs.

Barring The typical elongated areas of darker fur arranged randomly on the legs of most tabbies.

Binocular vision The way in which the visual fields from both eyes overlap in the center, to allow the brain to compute the exact position of prey, so that the cat can pounce with great accuracy.

Body language The way in which cats communicate with each other and their owners by nonverbal means, such as alterations in their body postures.

Booster A vaccination given after the primary course of vaccinations has been completed, to maintain protective cover. Boosters are usually required annually throughout the cat's life.

Breed standard A summary of what is deemed to be the ideal appearance of the cat of a particular breed, in terms of its conformation, coloration, and markings where appropriate.

Cat fancy The world of creating, breeding, and exhibiting purebred cats.

Cat flu A term usually applied to the main respiratory illnesses of cats, which are feline rhinotracheitis and feline calicivirus infection.

Catnip A herb that induces a feeling of well-being and euphoria in the majority of cats, although it has no effect on kittens.

Cattery A place where cats are kept, either for breeding or boarding purposes.

Colostrum The so-called "first milk" drunk by kittens that contains protective antibodies that can be absorbed directly into the body for the first few days of life.

Crossbreeding Mating of two different breeds of cats.

Dermatitis Inflammation and reddening of the skin, often seen in cases where a cat has developed a flea-bite allergy.

Diabetes mellitus A medical condition, often known as sugar diabetes, resulting from the malfunctioning of the pancreatic gland, which leads to an inadequate release of the hormone insulin.

Down hair The thinner hair underlaying the guard hairs, which provides insulation.

Ear mite A parasite localizing in the ear itself, which causes symptoms such as scratching and itching.

Estrus The period during which a female cat is receptive to tomcats.

Feline AIDS A viral infection that depresses the cat's immune system. It cannot be transmitted to people.

Feline Calcivirus (FCV) One of the viruses responsible for cat flu, which also often causes blistering of the tongue, making eating painful.

Feline Infectious Enteritis (FIE or Panleucopaenia) An infection that results in both a characteristic fall-off in the white blood cells (panleucopaenia) and enteritis. .

Feline Infectious Peritonitis (FIP) Infection of the abdomen, causing fever and weight loss. Usually affects younger cats.

Feline Viral Rhinotracheitis (FVR) The result of infection by a feline herpes virus, being another cause of cat flu, which is easily transmitted through sneezing at close-quarters.

Feral cat A cat descended from domestic stock that has reverted to a free-living existence.

Flehmening The way in which a cat will curl its top lip, to track down a scent, which registers via Jacobson's organ in the roof of the mouth.

Foreign A term used to describe a cat of Asian origins. Now only used specifically in the context of the Foreign White in Britain.

Furballs A mat of fur that can form in the cat's stomach, caused by the cat grooming itself with its rough tongue.

Gingivitis Inflammation of the gums, which may lead ultimately to loss of teeth in the affected area of the mouth.

Hybrid The offspring resulting from the breeding of two closely related species. It has given rise to the Bengal breed.

Hyoid Bony structure in throat area, at the base of the tongue.

Inoculation The administration of a vaccine.

Jowls The prominent fleshy folds of skin in mature male cats.

Kink An undesirable deviation in the tail, often associated with Siamese.

Lactase Enzyme responsible for the digestion of the milk sugar lactose. A deficiency is likely to lead to diarrhea in cats when they drink cow's milk.

Mackerel A distinctive type of tabby, with thin stripes running down the sides of its body.

Marbled A description applied to some Bengal cats, whose markings are said to resemble those of marble.

Molt Shedding of hair, typically as part of a seasonal cycle.

Muzzle The front of the cat's face, encompassing the jaws.

Neuter Surgery that is performed to prevent a cat from reproducing.

Parasite A creature that lives off a cat, bringing the cat no benefit, and frequently causing ill-health.

Pedigree The breeding lineage from which a particular cat is descended, as set down in a pedigree certificate.

Oriental A cat of Asiatic ancestry. It also refers to a popular group of shorthaired cats resembling Siamese, but which are solid-colored.

Ovulation The actual release of eggs from the ovary. In cats, this is triggered by the act of mating.

Pheromones Chemical messengers wafted on the wind, indicating that a queen is ready to mate.

Points The extremities of the body, comprising the face and ears, as well as the legs, feet, and tail. It is of significance in the case of pointed breeds such as the Siamese, where the fur is darker here than on the rest of the body.

Pot belly Swollen appearance toward the rear of the underside of the body. A pot belly indicates the heavy infestation by intestinal worms in kittens.

Purebred A cat that belongs to a particular breed.

Rabies A deadly viral disease transmitted through saliva. It can infect people as well as animals.

Recessive gene A gene that does not express itself visually when paired with the pure normal form but it can have harmful effects.

Rex Crimping of the hair in the coat.

Ringed Presence of rings around the tail of tabbies.

Ruff The longer area of fur around the neck of longhaired cats, which is especially prominent during the winter months.

Selective breeding A breeding program that is controlled, rather than allowing cats to mate randomly.

Spay To neuter a female cat.

Spotted Tabby pattern of markings, with spots predominating on the coat.

Stud cat A male cat kept for breeding purposes.

Tabby A cat that may display a series of darker blotches, ticking, stripes, or spots on its coat.

Tartar Deposit formed by food particles and associated bacteria on the gums and teeth.

Taurine An essential amino acid, derived from protein, which is necessary for good vision.

Territory An area occupied by a cat, which may seek to defend this space from incursions by others.

Ticked Alternating light and dark markings running down an individual hair. The Abyssinian breed is a typical example of a ticked tabby.

Toxoplasmosis A parasitic disease caused by microscopic protozoa, spread in cat feces.

Vaccinations A means of preventing disease by inoculations, injecting the cat with appropriate vaccines.

Valerian A herb valued for its calming effects especially for cats that become upset when travelling.

Weaning The process whereby a young cat starts to feed by itself, taking solid food rather than suckling.

Whiskers Specialized, thickened hairs occurring in clumps on the cat's head. They have a sensory function.

Worming The regular use of medication to overcome roundworms or tapeworms, which can parasitize the cat's intestinal tract.

Zoonoses Diseases such as rabies that can be spread from cats to people (and potentially vice versa).

useful addresses

Alley Cat Alleys
1801 Belmont Road NW, Suite 201
Washington DC 20009   Tel: (202) 667-3630

Website: http://www.alleycat.org

American Association of Cat Enthusiasts (AACE)
P.O. Box 213
Pine Brook
NJ 07058   Tel: (973) 335-6717

Website: http://www.aaceinc.org

American Cat Fanciers' Association (ACFA)
P.O. Box 203
MO 65726-0203   Tel: (417) 334-5430

Website: http://www.cats.org.uk

American Pet Association
P.O. Box 7172
Boulder CO 80306-7172   Tel: (800) 272-7387

Website: http://apa@apapets.org

American Society for the Prevention of Cruelty to Animals (ASPCA)
424 92nd St
NY 10128   Tel: (212) 876-7700

Website: http://www.aspca.org

National Association for Professional Pet Sitters
6 State Road (113)
Machanicsburg PA 17050   Tel: (717) 691-5565

Website: http://apa@apapets.org

The following lists the national and regional offices of the Humane Society of the United States, and the states they serve.

The Humane Society of the United States (DC, MD & VA)
2100 L Street, NW
Washington, DC 20037   Tel: (202) 452-1100

Website: http://www.hsus.org

Central States Regional Office (IL,KY, MN, NC, TN, WI)
800 West 5th Avenue, Suite 110
Naperville, IL 60563   Tel: (630) 357-7015

Great Lakes Regional Office (IN, MI, OH, WV)
745 Haskins Street
Bowling Green, OH 43402-1696   Tel: (419) 352-5141

Mid-Atlantic Regional Office (DE, NJ, NY, PA)
Bartley Square, 270 Route 206
Flanders, NJ 07836   Tel: (973) 927-5611

Midwest Regional Office (IA, KS, MO, NE)
1515 Linden Street
Suite 220
Des Moines, Iowa 50309   Tel: (515) 283-1393

New England Regional Office (CT, MA, ME, NH, RI)
Route 112, Halifax Jacksonville Town Line
Mailing address: P.O. Box 619
Jacksonville, VT 05342-0619   Tel: (802) 368-2790

Northern Rockies Regional Office (AK, ID, MT, ND, SD, WY)
490 North 31st Street, Suite 215
Billings, MT 59101   Tel: (406) 255-7161

Southeast Regional Office (AL, FL, GA, MS, SC)
1624 Metropolitan Circle, Suite B
Tallahassee, FL 32308   Tel: (850) 386-3435

Southwest Regional Office (AR, AZ, CO, LA, NM, OK, TX, UT)
3001 LBJ Freeway, Suite 224
Dallas, TX 75234   Tel: (972) 488-2964

West Coast Regional Office (CA, HI, NV, OR, WA)
5301 Madison Avenue, Suite 202
Mailing address: P.O. Box 417220
Sacramento, CA 95841-7220   Tel: (916) 344-1710

index

photography

All photographs (including cover) by Bruce Tanner
with the exception of the following:

Paul Harwood 7 top, 9 top right, 24 left, 27 top & right, 41 top, 47 right, 51 top & right, 59, 88 left, 90 both, 98, 107 middle right, 109 bottom right, 110 top, 111 bottom, 114, 121 top, 138, 139 bottom, 150 left, 158 bottom, 160/161 top, 161, 162 bottom right, 164 top, 165 all, 168 bottom.

Marc Henrie 1, 3, 5, 8, 17 top, 21 both, 22 top & middle, 23 both, 26, 27 bottom left, 28 left, 30 bottom left, 31 bottom, 34 bottom right, 36 bottom left and right, 39 right, 42, 43 centre right, 45 top left, 48 left, 49 top, 50, 55 bottom, 62 top, 66 bottom, 76 bottom, 85 bottom, 112, 117 top, 122 bottom, 125 right, 144.

Hodder Wayland Picture Library 53, 78 bottom left, 85 top, 91.

Illustrated London News 20 right.

Marion Ling 75 left, 115 bottom.

Mary Evans Picture Library 18 right, 19 left.

Linda Melbourne (Bluebell Ridge Cat's Home, Hastings) 58 top right, 99, 101, 106 top left, 115, 122 top, 123 top & bottom, 125, 126 left & middle, 127 right, 129 top.

Andy Rouse 6 left, 10, 13 right, 14 right, 15, 33.

Bob Schwartz (Excalibur) 28 right, 29 both.

Still Pictures 16, 18 left.

Artwork illustrations by
Patricia Clements 58, 104, 111, 116.
Alan Male 13, 113, 114, 115.
John Woodcock 32, 34, 39, 46, 59, 94, 102, 132, 143.

Special thanks

Special thanks to photographer Bruce Tanner and his cat, Sally the Stuntcat.

Thanks to the following people for photographic assistance, finding cats and modelling: Manon Droz, Sarah Maher, Jane and Oliver Anjos, Kathie Auton, Julie Cheriton, Colette and Alan, Josephine Doolan, Elaine Keating, Barbara Lawrence, Anastasia Lewis, Moira Millerick, Bob Tanner, Adrienne Truelove, Tina Watts, Clifford and Judith Dean, Diana Vowles and Wendy Helm.